THE TALE OF
BEATRIX POTTER

THE TALE OF BEATRIX POTTER

A Biography
MARGARET LANE

ISIS Large Print
Oxford

First published in Great Britain 1946 by Frederick Warne & Co. Ltd.

Published in Large Print by Clio Press Ltd, 55 St Thomas' Street, Oxford OX1 1JG, by arrangement with Penguin Books Ltd.

British Library Cataloguing in Publication Data

Lane, Margaret, *1907-*
    The tale of Beatrix Potter : a biography.
    1. Potter, Beatrix—Biography   2. Authors, English—20th century—Biography
    I. Title
    823'.912   PR6031.072Z/

ISBN 1-85089-086-2

Phototypeset, printed and bound by
Unwin Brothers Limited, Old Woking, Surrey.

Cover designed by CGS Studios, Cheltenham.

To my daughter
SELINA

ACKNOWLEDGMENTS

This life of Beatrix Potter, modest and unsensational though it is, could never have been written without the confidence and help of the late Mr. William Heelis, and the generous assistance of Beatrix Potter's family and friends. Without their aid, her biographer must have been entirely at a loss, for her life had been lived so privately, and was so carefully hidden from the public eye, that solitary research would have been all but fruitless. Mr. Heelis gave throughout the most valuable help, and placed many letters and photographs at my disposal, as well as his wife's portfolios and private papers.

Among the members of Beatrix Potter's own family who generously lent me letters and supplied information and personal recollections of her early life, I would like specially to remember her cousins, Miss Dora Roscoe and Mrs. Caroline Clark. Mr. and Mrs. W. F. Gaddum and Miss Eileen Bowen-Davis also gave valuable assistance, as did many of Beatrix Potter's correspondents and friends, notably Mrs. H. D. Rawnsley, Mrs. Annie Moore, the Rev. Noël Moore, Mrs. James Boultbee, Mrs. Fruing Warne, Miss E. L. Choyce, Miss Margaret Hammond, Miss Janet Adam Smith, Mr. and Mrs. Delmar Banner, Mr. Samuel Cunningham, Miss Bertha Mahony, Miss Helen Dean Fish, Miss Anne Carroll Moore and Miss Mary Gill.

Mr. Leslie Linder, to whose patient and brilliant work on *The Journal of Beatrix Potter* I owe so much, has my especial gratitude. Without his nine years' labour in transcribing that extraordinary document from code, much of the detail of Beatrix Potter's early life would have remained unknown.

The firm of Frederick Warne & Company has a special place in Beatrix Potter's life, and my debt is great to those members of it, especially Mr. Frederick Warne Stephens and the late Mr. W. A. Herring, who were her personal friends as well as her publishers, and who put their very large collection of letters at my service.

The officials of the National Trust (in particular the then Secretary Mr. D. M. Matheson, and Mr. B. L. Thompson) were uniformly sympathetic and helpful, and set before me the whole of Beatrix Potter's long correspondence with the Trust: I take this opportunity of thanking them. I owe much gratitude, too, to those Herdwick sheep-farmers and shepherds who gave me some little insight into their subject, and into Beatrix Potter's work as a breeder and farmer. In this connection it gives me real pleasure to mention with appreciation Mr. W. Wilson, Mr. George Walker, Mr. Thomas Storey, Mr. Thomas Stoddart, Mr. John Cannon and Mr. Joseph Moscrop.

M.L.

CONTENTS

INTRODUCTION

In Beatrix Potter's middle and old age not many people knew anything about her. Her name, of course, conjured up enchanting childhood memories of Peter Rabbit, Tom Kitten, Jemima Puddle-duck and the rest, but it was generally assumed that she had long been dead.

On the other hand, there was another person, a Mrs. William Heelis, wife of a solicitor in the Lake District, a woman well known locally as a farmer and shrewd purchaser of land, who could be bluntly outspoken at cattle shows and sheep fairs, and who pottered about in her own fields with a stout stick and usually, in wet and windy weather, a meal-sack across her shoulders. It was a fact known to remarkably few people that Beatrix Potter and Mrs. Heelis were one and the same.

This was precisely as she would have wished. She had lived her life through three very different phases, and her sense of personal privacy was extreme. Her childhood cannot be described as happy. Lonely, restricted, in the stuffy and frustrating atmosphere of a prosperous middle-class household in which almost any form of activity was frowned upon, she consoled herself with the company of small animals, chiefly mice and rabbits, which she loved and studied with the absorbing passion of both naturalist and artist. "I cannot rest," she wrote in the secret-code journal which she kept from her fourteenth to her thirtieth year, "I *must* draw, however poor the result ... I *will* do something sooner or later."

As indeed she did, passing into the second phase – only thirteen years – in which her picture-letters to the children of a former governess gradually developed into a series of little published masterpieces. Mrs. Tiggy-Winkle and the rest had partly fulfilled her creative urge, and – what seemed even more important at the time – had made her some money. So the foundations were laid for the final escape to freedom to a cottage of her own in the village of Sawrey, to a happy marriage in middle-age to the local solicitor who managed her property dealings, and to the life which truly satisfied her.

When I first visited the widowed William Heelis in Sawrey, after his reluctant consent that I might – *perhaps* – be allowed to write a discreet memoir of Beatrix Potter, I sensed her personality so strongly in every nook and cranny of the little house that it was difficult to believe that she was not still somewhere upstairs, dropping crumbs for the mice who crept out of the wainscot, warily suspicious of the voice she could hear from below.

"The imprint of her personality," I wrote in my diary that evening, after my long hours with Mr. Heelis, "was on every chair and table. Her clothes still hung behind the door, her geraniums trailed and bloomed along the window-sill, her muddles lay unsorted at one end of the table while he took his meals at the other, even a half-eaten bar of chocolate with her teeth-marks in it lay among the litter of letters on her writing-table."

To write her life, under the shadow of Mr. Heelis's loyal commitment to privacy and secrecy, was no easy matter;

but time was on my side, and in the end, with wonderful help from Potter cousins and friends, from the Warnes, her publishers for more than forty years, from farmers and shepherds and some of the children (now long grown-up) to whom those early proliferative letters had been written, the tale of Beatrix Potter, rather like a long-lost fairy-story, was at last told.

M.L.

CHAPTER
ONE

Bolton Gardens

i

The squares of Earl's Court and South Kensington, like those of Pimlico, have survived into the present day without much confidence. The tide of middle-class prosperity has receded, leaving the broad streets and Victorian houses a little shrunken. Some have retained their air of prosperity, others have not. There is a great deal of flaking paint and a preponderance of dustbins. A large part of the area has reached the shabby-genteel; its occasional beauty is due to the bloom of decay.

In the 'sixties and 'seventies of the last century it was very different. There were well-kept gardens and even the relics of orchards, and the houses were newer then; their steps were whitened each morning by housemaids in lilac print, tradesmen descended the area steps solicitously, and in the mews behind each solid front there were real carriages and coachmen. At regular hours ladies drove out in these carriages and left cards on one another, and the doors were opened by tall parlour-maids with streamers and even by butlers, and tea was drunk amid ferns and cushions in drawing-rooms, while the carriages waited.

All this, and more, could be seen by anyone who had

leisure and patience to watch from any of the upper windows of Bolton Gardens; and in the 'seventies, at the barred third-floor windows of the second house, there was stationed day after day a little girl who had leisure and solitude enough for the most prolonged study. She was solitary because she was an only child until she was five years old, and lived in a house which made no concessions to childhood; and she had limitless leisure because she was very rarely sent for out of the nursery or taken anywhere, and she never went to school. She had been born on 28 July 1866, and her name was Helen Beatrix Potter.

Number Two Bolton Gardens was very quiet. The ticking of the grandfather clock could be heard all over the house, like a slow heartbeat, and there were other reliable indications of the time of day. At the same hour every morning Mr. and Mrs. Rupert Potter came down to the dining-room for breakfast, a meal consumed in silence. Between ten and eleven Mr. Potter left for his club. At one o'clock a tray furnished with a small cutlet and a helping of rice pudding went up to the nursery by the back stairs, and as the clock struck two the carriage was at the door and Mrs. Potter, small and inflexibly upright and dressed in black, came down the whitened steps and got into it, and was driven away. At six o'clock Mr. Cox, the butler, could be observed through the dining-room windows preparing a solemn ritual with napkins and spoons and forks on the mahogany table. Soon the curtains would be drawn and the nursery lamp be extinguished, and to the street the house would give no further evidence of life.

In the same way, the seasons of the year could be judged with fair accuracy by even an indoor observer. Christmas, it is true, was not distinguished from an ordinary Unitarian

Sunday; but Easter meant a family exodus, generally to the seaside, lasting several weeks, while the servants spring-cleaned the house from top to bottom; and in summer the Potters and their servants removed in a body to a furnished house in Scotland, where Mr. Potter rented some shooting and fishing, and where gentlemen were invited. These Scottish holidays usually lasted for three months, and provided a long stretch of idleness and boredom for everyone except the servants, whose attention was focussed on the problem of reproducing the life of Bolton Gardens in a foreign setting – the one o'clock cutlet, the two o'clock drive for Mrs. Potter, then afternoon tea at five, followed by Mr. Cox's evening ceremonial of constructing cocked hats and water lilies out of table napkins.

Whether in London or in Scotland, life as the Rupert Potters understood it held little to interest the solitary child upstairs, and it would perhaps have surprised them if anyone had suggested that life might conceivably be made interesting to one so young. She was provided with a Scottish nurse of Calvinistic principles; she had a clean starched piqué frock every morning and "cotton stockings striped round and round like a zebra's legs"; a cutlet and rice pudding came up the back stairs every day for lunch, and in the afternoon, unless it rained, McKenzie the nurse took her for a good walk. What more could a child want? Nothing, perhaps; for quiet, solitary and observant children create their own world and live in it, nourishing their imaginations on the material at hand; and she was not at all unhappy. Did not Ruskin, as a child, have as his sole plaything a bunch of keys? The child Beatrix Potter had more, much more; she had "a dilapidated black wooden doll called Topsy, and a very grimy, hard-stuffed, once-white flannelette pig", which did not belong to her, but

which was brought out on special occasions from the
bottom drawer of her grandmother's *secrétaire*; and the
house contained the Waverley novels, on which she
learned to read, and the complete works of Miss Edge-
worth; and she composed hymns and "sentimental ballad
descriptions of Scottish scenery", and in her unmolested
upper storey constructed a child's defence against the
airless grown-up life which went on below, and which
seemed to have no idea of evoking response, and which
certainly offered her nothing.

She had been born into a period and a class which seem
to have had little understanding of childhood. Her parents
were rich, both of them being the possessors of Lancashire
cotton fortunes; but they were removed by at least a
generation from the hard-headed Lancashire vigour which
had made those fortunes; and being a well-to-do married
couple of the 'seventies, not "in society", no longer personally contaminated by trade and not active in any profession,
they had fallen without knowing it under the most ener-
vating and stultifying influence of their century – the
sterile spell of moneyed and middle-class gentility.

It is not quite true to say that Rupert Potter had no
profession. He had been called to the Bar, and described
himself as a barrister; but he had never practised, since
the only brief he had ever received had turned out to be
a hoax – a discovery which he made with great relief. But
after all, what need was there to work? He had plenty of
money, and although there was a certain dignity in being
a barrister, to renounce the actual toil of the profession
was even more becoming in a gentleman. So Mr. Potter
made a life for himself, and lived it punctually. He spent
much time at the Athenaeum and Reform Clubs, where
he read the newspapers; he paid afternoon visits, and

perfected a dry querulous ironical style of anecdote which served for conversation; and he came out strong as an amateur photographer.

It was an age of pioneer photography; the invention was still young, the equipment expensive; and Mr. Potter, though he seems to have lacked the artist's eye which produced so many beautiful Victorian photographs, achieved at least a high level of technical excellence. He took views of Scottish scenery, he photographed trees, he arranged serious groups on the steps of country houses, he made portrait studies of Mrs. Potter (who often received compliments on her likeness to Queen Victoria) pausing to reflect against a background of conifers, or resting her gloved hand on a rustic post. More interesting still, he took his apparatus on certain afternoons to Mr. Millais' studio, and photographed the artist's sitters in the pose in which they were being painted, thus combining the pleasures of his hobby with performing a useful service for a friend. ("Mr. Millais says the professionals aren't fit to hold a candle to Papa.") In this way he made an interesting collection of portraits, of which his study of Gladstone – severe, eagle-eyed, putting on the elder statesman with just a shade too keen a sense of personal drama – is probably the best. There is a family tradition that Millais offered, in return, to paint the rosy little girl he had caught a glimpse of on one of his return visits to Bolton Gardens. Her cousin Kate Potter, a remarkably beautiful child, had sat to Rivière for a sentimental nursery picture called *Cupboard Love*, but Mr. Potter is said to have refused to have Beatrix painted because it might make her vain.

Beatrix herself, more than twenty years later, admitted in her secret journal that she had been "unmercifully afraid of [Millais] as a child . . . I had a brilliant colour as a little girl, which he used to provoke on purpose and remark upon at times. If a great portrait painter's criticism is of any interest this is it . . . that I was a little like his daughter Carrie, at that time a fine handsome girl, but my face was spoiled by the length of my nose and upper lip."

Personal vanity was frowned on in the Potter household, and Beatrix, though she was a pretty child and afterwards a distinctly attractive woman, seems never to have felt the least temptation to it. She submitted patiently to the starching and brushing and tying up with ribbons, the lacing of boots and the carrying of muffs, which was a part of well-to-do childhood in the 'seventies; but she was never beguiled. It was something to escape from, when one should be old enough, a part of that stagnant life which went on in the drawing-room, and which laid it down that little girls, except when they were in pinafores, should be booted and dressed as though they were going to church.

Church-going, as it happened, was less rigidly insisted on in the Potter household than in many Church of England families, for both Mr. and Mrs. Potter were Unitarians, and possessed a fair degree of the tolerance, if not the intellectualism, of their sect. They went to various Unitarian churches, and "sat under" this minister or that; but the religious atmosphere of the household was not oppressive, and their children (for by the time that Beatrix was old enough to go to church she had a brother) were allowed to grow up in the belief that one might, without spiritual injury, enjoy a simple religious service of any denomination, provided it were plain. In their religious faith, as in their lives, the Potters were calm, avoiding the vulgar enthusiasms which had made their forebears interesting; for Mr. Potter, at least, had had remarkable parents, his father having been a self-made man of the best type, and a reformer, and his mother (who died at the age of ninety, when Beatrix was twenty-five) being a Crompton, which meant that there was something about her which was full of character and oddity, and which made her, in the eyes of an impressionable child, a fascinating grandmother.

Rupert Potter was extremely proud of his father, not because he was a self-made man – that, perhaps, least of all – but because he had been Liberal M.P. for Carlisle and a friend of Cobden and Bright, and had died in possession of more money than he knew what to do with. He was, in fact, an attractive and remarkable person, a reformer as well as an industralist, one of those clear-sighted, humane and science-loving Victorians who made it easy for the age to believe in its own progress. He had been born in Manchester in 1802, into a poor family with a respect for education. His early life had been hard, but not unrewarding; he had taken his decent education and his integrity into the calico-printing trade, and to such good effect that in middle-age, owner of the Dinting Vale Works at Glossop and a magistrate, he had found himself at the head of the new industry. His rise had not been easy, but he had never been afraid of work, and had driven himself to stringent efforts in the face of adversity. In the 'thirties, about the time that his son Rupert was born, the calico-printing trade had had reverses, and Edmund Potter's firm had failed, and he had gone bankrupt. Almost without a pause he had begun again, going back to manual labour and small beginnings; and in the course of the next ten years, with north-country pride of honesty, had paid back all his creditors to the last farthing and was already on the upward slope to fortune.

Yet he was not at all a harsh man; indeed, his life was largely spent in trying to propagate and share among his fellows those advantages which had helped to make him successful. As a poor boy he had profited by education; in Parliament he made popular education his chief concern. Himself a Dissenter (for he had been brought up and remained a strong Unitarian, one of that ethical-intellectual Manchester group which centred in the Gaskells) he campaigned for religious equality and toleration. He was a Radical, a free-trader, a humane magistrate, a delighted spectator of the progress of science, an amateur of the arts. And perhaps because he was also handsome, in the blue-eyed, strong-featured, gentle intellectual mode which speaks to us with such delighting frequency from the daguerreotypes of the period, he had married a woman of beauty and spirit, that same Jessie Crompton who was to provide the first mental stimulus for her small grand-daughter, Beatrix.

ii

Beatrix's grandmother, Mrs. Edmund Potter, knew what life was composed of, and she distilled it, drop by drop, never generously, never deliberately, but at least without fraud or censure, in leisurely reminiscent conversations to which the child, seated on a cross-bar underneath the library table and hidden by the green fringed cloth, could surreptitiously listen. There was much that she heard in this earliest, under-the-table stage of listening to her grandmother that she did not follow; nor did she attend much at first, having adopted this sanctuary not at all, really, for the purpose of listening, but in order to nurse the flannelette pig in peace, and to eat the hard ginger-snap biscuits which her grandmother gave her privately from a canister, and on which, one by one, she loosened her milk teeth. But even on these earliest visits to Camfield Place, the hideous but very comfortable yellow brick country house which Edmund Potter had adapted for himself near Hatfield, the name of Crompton was dropped so often into the conversation, and with such emphasis, that it acquired a special potency, and drew her gradually into a charmed attentiveness to the reminiscences of her Potter grandmother.

By the time Beatrix was ten years old, and, though very small for her age, too big to sit without eccentricity under the table, her grandmother was already an old lady of seventy-five, dressed always in rich black silk with a white shawl, white cotton stockings, a white cap with black velvet ribbons, and mittens. Yet in spite of these trappings of old ladyhood, and her three grey corkscrew ringlets on either cheek, it was still possible when her brown eyes sparkled, as they did very often and in the liveliest manner, to imagine the vanished beauty which had made her a toast, and had even caused her (or so she said) to be mobbed in the streets of Lancaster. To say that in youth one was mobbed for one's beauty is a bold claim. To be stared at, yes; to be admired, to have three proposals in a week and be the envy of the ballroom – all these have a flavour of possibility, and an accepted place in the recollections of grandmothers. But to believe in mobbing one must imagine a crowd gathered and the way barred, rude yet honest Lancashire faces thrusting and peering, a delicious terror and embarrassment which few women who are not celebrated actresses ever know. Yet one must also remember that Mrs. Edmund Potter was a Unitarian, and had been well brought up. Great were the battles, she told Mrs. Rupert, which as a girl she had waged against her non-Unitarian schoolfellows, "for the faith". And the Cromptons, who were an arrogant lot and given to extravagant expressions of opinion in politics and ethics, were also proud of their hard-headed cautiousness in matters of fact. So the beautiful Jessie Crompton was conceded, in her husband's family, that romantic mobbing; the more easily, perhaps, since she never claimed it wholly for herself, but was always careful to share the glory with one or other of her eight sisters.

There were other stories which Beatrix, now sitting up to the oval table itself (for her grandmother did not permit young people to sit in armchairs or loll about at random) with book or needlework before her, felt that she must remember, even to the words that her grandmother used and the tone of her voice. Ostensibly busy drawing butterflies, she began to record her talk on odd sheets of paper, using a self-invented secret writing which was partly an ingenious code, partly a script so small that (as with the Brontës' childhood manuscripts) no inquisitive grown-up, unless prepared to go the length of using a magnifying glass, could see what it was. Worth remembering, for instance, was the sad story of one of Grandmama's earliest admirers, who had drowned himself for love in a lily pond. He had written a poem beginning "Sweet harp of Lune Villa!" – a charming line, suggestive of northern summer evenings and the nine Miss Cromptons sitting in the drawing-room in their Regency muslins, with the windows open, and the beautiful Miss Jessie at the instrument. But Grandmama could remember no more than that opening apostrophe, "Then he made away with himself . . ." It was dreadfully sad, and surprising, too, when you came to think of it. (There were disloyal suggestions from other branches of the family that his death had been an accident.) Perhaps, then, he had been haunting the garden of Lune Villa in the dark, yearning at the drawing-room windows and listening to the harp, and had taken a rapt step backwards against the stone margin of the pool, so that there had been a cry and a dreadful splash, and the harp had faltered for a moment while the nine Miss Cromptons listened . . .

Equally harsh, but less harrowing, was the fate of another lover who attended the same chapel and sat under the same minister as the Radical and Unitarian Cromptons. "Quite a common man," said Grandmama dispassionately, "one of the congregation. My mother directed the footman to put him under the pump." Beatrix herself in the last year of her life rediscovered these childish pages, and deciphered this anecdote with a less simple amusement than she had felt at twelve years old. "Alas," she wrote in the margin, "alas for the rights of man and universal equality!" For the Cromptons, despite their summary methods with social inferiors, were themselves great Radicals and individualists, and prided themselves on the amount of trouble they had managed to get into (in spite of their wealth) in the eighteenth and early nineteenth centuries. "Oh, we were such Radicals in those days!" said Grandmama Potter, gazing into the fire as her granddaughter's pencil moved silently over the page. "Those days" were early in the century, for she well remembered the national mourning for Princess Charlotte, and had been walking with her governess in the streets of Liverpool when "we heard of Waterloo". (These scraps of code writing, microscopic and mysterious, eventually developed into a voluminous secret journal which Beatrix kept until she was past thirty.)

The Cromptons, for as far back as they could be traced, had always been men of character and arrogant conscience – substantial yeomen, rich farmers, country bankers, cotton spinners and merchants, embedding themselves from time to time like sharp flints in the undercrust of smaller Lancashire gentry. "I am descended," wrote Beatrix Potter in old age to an American friend who had asked for particulars of her descent, "from generations of Lancashire yeomen and weavers; obstinate, hard-headed, matter-of-fact folk ... As far back as I can go they were Puritans, Nonjurors, Nonconformists, Dissenters. Your *Mayflower* ancestors sailed to America; mine at the same time were sticking it out at home, probably rather enjoying persecution." The male Cromptons certainly seem to have relished persecution, or at least the thought of it, for their Radicalism was of the argumentative rather than the practical variety, and Grandmama Potter's father, Abraham Crompton, seems to have been the only one who suffered at all publicly for his opinions. Grandmama remembered something about it, and also about the moral courage of one of her uncles, and spoke of these things with a mild detached satisfaction, laying great stress on the fact that she was a Crompton herself, and a Potter only by marriage. "I remember my Uncle Crompton at Eton; he hid a man in his house – one that would have been hung. And my father was just as bad. It was about the time of the Manchester Massacre ... about 1819. You know, he was taken off the Bench of Magistrates because he went to see a man who was in the Castle. He did not care about persecution, but my mother did. She did not like it."

The man whom Abraham Crompton visited in prison

was Thistlewood, the Cato Street conspirator, who had learned his revolutionary theories in Paris and had dedicated himself on his return to England to the manufacture of hand grenades and the study of strategy. After several attempts to organize an English revolution, and several consequent imprisonments, he decided in 1820 on a *coup d'état* which was to be both original and decisive. The Cabinet was to be assassinated at dinner with a bomb, Coutts's Bank razed, public buildings in the City set on fire, the Tower seized, and a provisional government set up in the Mansion House with a cobbler called Ings as secretary. The thorough-going spirit of this programme seems for some reason to have appealed to Crompton, who took it into his head, after Thistlewood had been arrested in his Cato Street arsenal, to champion the man's cause and quarrel with his fellow magistrates. He even went the length of visiting the conspirator in prison, to encourage and console; but without happy results. Thistlewood was hanged and Crompton removed from the Bench.

Grandmama could not remember if her father had ever been to France, to account for the surprising warmth of his revolutionary sympathies. She thought perhaps he must have done, for he had some odd tastes in food, and used as a very old man to wander out into the grounds of Lune Villa on damp summer evenings in search of snails, which he liked prepared with butter and chopped parsley, and ate with a pin.

He seems to have enjoyed his Radicalism, however, chiefly because it supported the Crompton reputation for crustiness, for in spite of his expressed sympathy with Thistlewood's principles he liked to see his wife and thirteen children living in style, being no hater of private property, and indeed fond of adding to his own when the profits of the cotton trade allowed it. He had inherited Chorley Hall in Lancashire (which had originally been bought by his great-grandfather, another Abraham Crompton, from the Crown) but had sold this property while Grandmama was still a girl, and bought Lune Villa. He also bought land "for pleasure" in the Lake District, a small farm in a fold of Tilberthwaite Fell, where he and his family repaired for a few weeks in the summer. And Grandmama remembered that there were other farming properties, too, bought for profit; and had a dreamlike recollection of driving with her father in a gig across Lancaster Sands to pay for a rich farm that he was buying. In this anecdote, half memory, half dream, which Beatrix remembered all her life with peculiar pleasure, the moon had been rising and the tide had been coming in rapidly over the wide sands; and Grandmama had been nervous, and wished that the horse would go faster, and had clasped the bag of purchase money – all gold, and very heavy – in her lap.

iii

The earlier Abraham Crompton of Chorley Hall – "old Abr'am" as he was known in the family – was a far greater figure in the Crompton legend than Grandmama's father. Even Rupert Potter, who disliked exertion but inherited his mother's passion for dwelling on the obscure details of their genealogies, spent a good deal of time in writing letters and consulting Unitarian chapel registers to find out more about this interesting ancestor. He was always spoken of as though he were the originator of the

Crompton character, of which they were all so proud; as if, at least, the stamp of his peculiar nature had been so deep that the impress, now fainter, now sharper, could be traced and recognized in all succeeding generations, and might even – or so Beatrix believed – throw up a shadowy suggestion of pattern in herself. "I am a believer in breed," she wrote in old age, looking back over her own life and taking pleasure in those rugged features of personal landscape which she believed were due, even at this distance of time, to eruptions of old Abr'am, "I hold that a strongly marked personality can influence descendants for generations. In the same way that we farmers know that certain sires – bulls, stallions, rams – have been prepotent in forming breeds of shorthorns, thoroughbreds, and the numerous varieties of sheep . . . The most remarkable old character amongst my ancestors was old Abraham Crompton."

Neither Rupert Potter nor his mother, nor even Beatrix herself when she was old enough to inherit the genealogical passion, was ever able to find out very much about him. Yet the legend of his personality was still strong after a hundred years, which would seem to support their conception of him as a forceful, crusty, out-spoken, common-sense eccentric. The important thing about the Crompton legend, so far as it affected Beatrix, was that she grew up with an admiration for these qualities. For in spite of the paralysing conventionality of Bolton Gardens and the absolute rigidity of their lives, the Potters had an almost eighteenth-century respect for wealthy eccentricity, and liked to find unexpected quirks of behaviour here and there among their ancestors; liked to think, for instance, that a Potter had married a daughter of Bradshaw the regicide (there was a table-cloth belonging to Bradshaw somewhere in the family) and that Chorley Hall itself had been involved in two rebellions.

Old Abr'am's connection with the '45 provided the most amusing story that was known about him, and it was all the more fascinating to a child because it was a story with relics which might be seen and handled – a few large linen table-napkins with the royal arms of Scotland woven into them and "C. P." embroidered in cross-stitch near one of the borders. The first Abraham Crompton, who was a banker and lived in Derby, had bought Chorley Hall from the Crown in 1715, thus taking his initial step into the landed gentry. He bought it for something over five thousand pounds. "I had imagined that the Chorley Hall estate was more important and expensive," Rupert Potter wrote with some disappointment when his researches brought this financial detail to light; but its cheapness was perhaps partly due to its being forfeited property – Richard Chorley, the owner, having been taken at Preston and beheaded for his support of the Old Pretender in 1715.

The Cromptons were rebel-fanciers, but not of the royalist order; they had no sentimental weakness for the Stuarts, and indeed, as Dissenters and nonjurors had a special abhorrence of Catholics, divine right of kings, oaths of allegiance, romantic emotion, French influences, gallantry, dressing up, and everything connected with that most poetic and hopeless of lost causes. Old Abr'am may well, therefore, have felt some virtuous satisfaction in acquiring cheaply the property of a gentleman so very justly disgraced as Richard Chorley; and for thirty years he enjoyed his new possession in his own way, briskly bringing Chorley into line with the Crompton tradition and reclaiming the place with the stamp of Puritan respectability.

In '45, however, the Young Pretender landed in the Hebrides, and with what at first seemed supernatural success made his bold way south, capturing Carlisle and arriving eventually at Lancaster. Here, remembering very probably that his father had had kind treatment from Richard Chorley, who had fought and died for him, he rode at once with his army to Chorley Hall, and clattered up to the gate with the royal standard flying and supported by a retinue of famished Highlanders. The Chorley villagers, respectable wary Dissenters though they mostly were, had no option but to receive them, and Crompton dared not refuse hospitality to the Prince, who stayed the night and dined in excellent spirits, providing his own silver and table linen.

One cannot help wondering how the honest Radical conducted himself during that memorable evening. One would like to hear that he had been bidden to the royal table, and to know how he emerged from the struggle between vanity and principle. But there is no family tradition that he sat down with Prince Charlie, nor is there any Cromptonish anecdote of refusal; so the most probable conclusion is, after all, that he was not asked, but simply instructed to place his kitchen and cellar at the Pretender's disposal, and then left to mutter in the passages. That there were grounds for muttering seems undeniable, for the Presbyterian minister at Chorley, on whom thirty-six of the rebels were quartered, has left it on record that they consumed forty-one pounds of his best cheese while waiting for their dinner – a *cri du cœur* from the manse which still has power to move us after two centuries. The only known gesture of retaliation which was made at Chorley was the theft of a handful of spade guineas and the Prince's marked table napkins, which were hidden under a loose floorboard at the Hall – by whom or for what purpose nobody knows. They were found many years later, when the floor was taken up in the course of some repairs, and the presumption was that they had been hidden by a dishonest servant. One exonerates Crompton himself without a second glance; he would have scorned the theft, however much of his cheese they might have eaten; and one cannot see him, somehow, collecting Stuart relics.

It was very puzzling, and the Potters never quite knew how to account for the napkins and the guineas. The napkins alone might have suggested a secret attachment to the Pretender's cause – a laundry-maid's liking for a bonny face, or hidden Stuart loyalties in the breast of a footman. But the presence of the spade guineas destroys this idyll. Guineas are rarely prized for their sentimental value, and one can accept the romantic explanation only by admitting as well (as one certainly should) that motives are generally mixed. That the napkins and guineas were stolen for different reasons seems the likeliest theory, and in support of it there is the curious fact that the guineas vanished soon after their discovery, while the napkins remained as relics in the Potter family.

CHAPTER
TWO

Summer Holidays

i

Beatrix Potter believed in heredity, and in later life was often amused by what she regarded as outcroppings of native Crompton rock in her own character; and it should be remembered (by those who dismiss heredity in favour of environment) that in her lonely, circumscribed and mentally airless childhood the Crompton legend had been consistently presented to her as something admirable; and that she had listened through many idly receptive hours to her grandmother's conversation, from which it emerged that a certain ruggedness of character, outspokenness, shrewd argumentative common sense and indifference to appearances were qualities to be smiled at and admired. One by one, and as soon as she dared, she developed all of them.

Her parents seem not to have noticed that she was unnaturally lonely. Her brother Bertram, when he was old enough, disappeared to school, and she had no other friends. She knew no neighbourhood children, and was given no opportunity of knowing any. Even cousins (and she had her share of these, notably Kate and Blanche Potter, a little older than herself and much livelier and prettier) though they sometimes came to Bolton Gardens with their parents, never became intimates. She neither shared her parents' life nor mixed with other children.

One result of these strange years of seclusion was that she became exceedingly shy, and was tongue-tied and *farouche* on the rare occasions when she found herself in company. Yet she was not unhappy. One prefers, as a rule, what one is accustomed to, and she had grown to like her third-floor solitude, which was rarely interfered with and had at least the advantages of privacy. She did not mind being alone; nothing had ever happened to make her afraid of it; and it was remembered by at least one contemporary cousin that she was immune from the bedtime terrors of the hall at Camfield Place, where marble busts of Gladstone, Cobden, Bright and Peel glimmered like phantoms, and where she went undismayed about the dark stairs and passages. This complete resistance to superstitious suggestion, unusual in a girl of her age and period, became a marked feature of her character, and is unconsciously illustrated by one of those scraps of description which survived in a forgotten corner of a cupboard until her last years, when she discovered a bundle of cipher-written fragments dating from adolescence. "We sat upon the green velvet sofa hand in hand, looking at the log fire in the drawing-room ... waiting for dinner. I dressed early and then sat beside Grandmama while other people were dressing. The room was lighted exclusively by very tall wax candles. I remember an occasion when every one of those candles – six of them, doubtless from one defective box – went out, calmly and without spluttering. Some people might not have liked it. My grandmother without comment desired the bell to be rung for fresh candles."

In this direction, loneliness was to do her sturdy temperament no damage, though it was to leave other marks upon her. In her long captivity on the third floor of Bolton Gardens ("my unloved birthplace", as she wrote of it in old age, when she heard it had been destroyed by bombing in 1940) she had withdrawn her attention from the life of the house, and turned it with intense focus on her own fantasies and interests, and on a strong affection for her governess. Miss Hammond's period in the schoolroom was a happy one. She seems to have been a woman of great gentleness and delicacy of spirit, who encouraged the child's awakening interest in nature and in drawing, and gave her that feeling of loving confidence in an older presence which she might otherwise have missed. But Miss Hammond's reign was not a long one; she left apparently during Beatrix's early teens, protesting that the child had already far outstripped her, and that she could teach her nothing. Undisturbed by any hankerings for school or higher education, Beatrix continued her hermit existence in the nursery, busy with her own concerns. "Thank goodness, my education was neglected; I was never sent to school ... The reason I am glad I did not go to school – it would have rubbed off some of the originality (if I had not died of shyness or been killed with over pressure). I fancy I could have been taught anything if I had been caught young; but it was in the days when parents kept governesses, and only boys went to school in most families."

Though it was in the London schoolroom that she developed unexpected tastes, it was not there that she acquired them. Her imagination had been first awakened during those early Scottish holidays, which the Potters had done their best to make as boring as Bolton Gardens, but which nevertheless, for Beatrix and her brother, provided their first experience of freedom. To both children, taken for the first time beyond the London streets, contact with fields and flowers and hedgerow animals, with the sights and smells and labours of cottages and farms, came as a pure revelation of what was interesting and *real*. "It sometimes happens," she wrote when she was seventy, "that the town child is more alive to the fresh beauty of the country than a child who is country born. My brother and I were born in London ... But our descent, our interests and our joy were in the north country."

Beatrix had always, from her earliest years, had a strong sense of the unreality of Bolton Gardens, servants, formality, "manners", routine, the endless stony plains of boredom that these things implied, were conditions to be endured with fortitude, since they belonged to the way of life her parents accepted; but to herself she had always admitted her impatience. The Scottish holidays, with their ravishing natural discoveries, gave her a basis of comparison; and from the first moment of wandering out into the lanes and fields her imagination found the food it had been waiting for. Everything that she saw was suddenly "real". Farms and cottages were real. Animals were real. Even the frog captured for a moment among the stones of a stream or the wood-mouse washing its whiskers under a leaf, led interesting and reasonable lives according to their conditions. They were beautiful to look at, too; mysterious, full of surprises, intent on their small concerns with a completeness which allowed her, crouched in a trance of stillness among the ferns, to share their lives for the space of long summer afternoons, and to understand, as a child's imagination can, what it feels like to thread one's way under the grass and bracken. This vision of the beauty and integrity of wild life, on however tiny a scale, was peculiarly clear, and still kept its freshness and innocence of eye as she grew older. A "precocious and tenacious memory" preserved it, unclouded and unchanged. "I have been laughed at for what I say I can remember; but it is admitted that I can remember quite plainly from one and two years old; not only facts, like learning to walk, but places and sentiments – the way things impressed a very young child."

The things which impressed her most were the things she had never known in her London life. Not only the child's half-real, half-fantastic world of pond and ditch, stone walls and fox-gloves, woods and sandy warrens, but the farm-yard and the human scene as well. Here, in white-washed cottages and among rick-yards, whole families lived in a way which her instinct told her was sensible and right. If her later theories of heredity were true, it was perhaps some homely practical north-country strain in her, something from much further back than Lancashire cotton-spinning or old Abr'am's rise to gentility, which responded so instantly, with such a sense of coming home, to the sight of a flagged floor and a kitchen range, to a pan of dough rising under an old clean blanket beside the hearth, to cupboards and dressers full of a jumble of crockery, pelargoniums in the deep recesses of parlour windows, and crowded cottage gardens planted without formality or plan and blooming with pinks and snapdragons and sage and parsley, all flourishing together. She noticed everything. The knobs on a cupboard door, the well-trodden rag rug before the high steel fender, the cool stone-and-water smell of the dairy, the empty mouse-trap kicked aside in a corner. This was how farmers lived, and it was perfect. She went round the barns and rick-yards with a basket, helping to collect the eggs; she took out a bowl of grain to the poultry, and fed the ducklings on soft mash with a wooden spoon. She made friends with the farm collies, and found she was not afraid of them; the calves in the byre, even the pigs in their sty had more to say to her, were more responsive and understandable than grown-up people. And there was certainly a magic air about these Scottish holidays, for even McKenzie, the correct, the inflexible, the lover of starched piqué, became strangely unlike her London self, and remembered fairy stories. She had heard about witches and enchantments, and half believed in them, and though she still administered her dose of Calvinism on the Sabbath, the fairies kept creeping into her talk in the most unsabbatical manner. Beatrix, misleadingly steady of eye and stolid of expression, absorbed it all – "the firm belief in witches, fairies and the creed of the terrible John Calvin. The creed," she afterwards reflected, "rubbed off, but the fairies remained." Remained, but with this difference; that it was not McKenzie's goblins and spirits that her imagination welcomed, so much as the poetic freedom to project her own fantasies on to the animal kingdom. "I do not remember a time when I did not try to invent pictures and make for myself a fairyland amongst the wild flowers, the animals, fungi, mosses, woods and streams, all the thousand objects of the countryside; that pleasant unchanging world of realism and romance, which in our northern clime is stiffened by hard weather, a tough ancestry, and the strength that comes from the hills."

ii

Like most healthy children, she and her brother were not squeamish, and there was a toughness about some of their experiments which would have surprised their parents, accustomed only to seeing them in the drawing-room, or, meekly booted and pinafored, accompanying elderly visitors round the garden. They decided to make a collection of all the plants, animals and insects they could find, and smuggled home innumerable beetles, toadstools, dead birds, hedgehogs, frogs, caterpillars, minnows and sloughed snakeskins. If the dead specimen were not past skinning, they skinned it; if it were, they busily boiled it and kept the bones. They even on one occasion, having obtained a dead fox from heaven knows where, skinned and boiled it successfully in secret and articulated the skeleton. (One wonders in what secluded outhouse this research was carried out; it was not likely to meet with sympathy from McKenzie or Mrs. Potter.) And everything that they brought home, they drew and painted. They sewed together little drawing books out of odd sheets of paper and filled them with drawings of birds' eggs, flowers, and butterflies. From babyhood Beatrix had had a passion for paint-box and pencil, and her earliest drawings had nearly all been of animals and birds, copied from plates in old-fashioned natural histories – kingfishers, eagles, humming-birds, hippopotamuses, things she had never seen. Now the little books were filled with rabbits, cows, sheep, caterpillars, cottages, a leaf or two, a sprig of wallflower, a view of a dairy. Realistic enough for the most part, and as careful of detail as a child naturalist of ten years old can be; but here and there on the grubby pages fantasy breaks through – mufflers appear round the necks of newts, rabbits walk upright, skate on ice, carry umbrellas, walk out in bonnets and mantles like Mrs. Potter's.

The two of them not only drew every natural object they could lay their hands on, they discovered an obsolete printing press, "a hand press with an agonising squeak", and made elementary wood-cuts. The press had been joyfully stumbled on in a lumber room, complete, more or less, but without ink. They made their own from soot and colza oil – "a sticky black mess, always either too thick or too thin, mixed on a board and applied to the type with a small roller ... I can hear it squeak, and always the type wrenched sideways." In the hope of obtaining grown-up sanction for the new printing business they proffered a few artistic labels for jam pots; but "the ink was so messy it was confiscated."

Anything messy, however interesting, was still forbidden, and the best experiments were those that could be carried out in private. The Scottish holidays, fruitful and rewarding though they were, had not been undertaken for the amusement of children, but chiefly to provide an interest and a change for Mr. Potter. The Potters did not entertain at Bolton Gardens, and indeed it is hard to imagine what would attract visitors to that particular house, described as it has been by an irreverent Potter cousin as "a dark Victorian mausoleum, complete with aspidistras"; but at the comfortable country houses which he rented first in Scotland and then in the Lake District Mr. Potter was able to hold out bait in the way of shooting or fishing to one or two Unitarian ministers (Mr. Gaskell, whose fascinating wife had died some years before, was a frequent guest) and sometimes to a friend of his father's, like the Quaker orator and statesman, John Bright, who was a devout fisherman. Bright was perhaps the most attractive of the Potters' visitors. He was an old man now, almost as white as his marble bust at Camfield Place; but he still enjoyed the company of children, and still possessed his beautiful orator's voice. "He liked to read poetry aloud. It seems to me looking back that he sometimes read poetry that was scarcely worthy of the voice. I do remember his reading some Milton, but he would good-naturedly read any minor poet who came to hand. His voice was low-pitched, but magnificent ... a great man, impressive to a child."

Fishing was not allowed on Sundays, and so, if the day were fine, taking Beatrix and Bertram with him, the old man would walk as far as Stewartfield, "an old dower house hidden in the fold of the moor, in a stunted wood", where he would ask the caretaker to unlock a particular cupboard and let him handle a little harp that had belonged to Mary Queen of Scots. There were other things here, too, to fascinate the children: a curious carved pillar supporting a unicorn, and some uncouth unexplained statues on the stone terrace. "They were stumpy figures about four foot high, presumably mythological – they had very little on. Their workmanship was so crude and unlifelike that nobody with a sense of humour would have found them embarrassing. But the old Scotch gardener abhorred them – 'them stukky figgers' he called them ... He trained and clipped honeysuckle to encage their nakedness, so that their heads looked out from green mantles of leaves ... One goddess used to have a fly-catcher's nest in her bosom every summer, under the honeysuckle flowers."

Together with Mr. Bright they studied, but could not explain, another oddity. "Beyond the ancient buttressed garden wall were potting sheds, rubbish heaps, and a wet untidy wood, planted with spruce. Some attempt had been made to drain the outskirts of the wood, but in the centre there were strange bankments which even to the eyes of an observant child were mysterious zigzag ridges and ditches, miniature earthworks. Too large to be the work of the wondrous and indefatigable ant; too symmetrical to be excavated by rabbits; too muddy and messy to be made by the fairies (in whom I then believed). On the whole I took them to be a misdirected work of grown-ups, either a small-scale model of a fortification after the manner of 'my Uncle Toby', or a play after the manner of Edie Ochiltree, or by the planters and drainers who had laid out the spruce foundation. These curious little banks and ditches remained a puzzle of childhood and a perplexing memory for many years. I now realise that it was in fact a great rarity and curiosity – an old maze."

Less impressive than Mr. Gaskell and less congenial than John Bright, but still good value in his way, was Sir William Brown, another visiting fisherman, whose passion seems to have swamped his conversation. (He had, indeed, only one reminiscence that was not to do with fish: he had seen Sir Walter Scott with his own eyes – "he remembered to have seen Sir Walter walking along Princes Street; a man that men turned to look after; a lame man walking rather hurriedly.") But his fishing stories were worth hearing because they were accompanied by so much action and were the source of so much annoyance to Mr. Cox. "He could catch salmon on hopeless days and in hopeless places – even on the bridge and promenade of his native town ... But no salmon that he caught were comparable

31

with the stories of salmon which he had played and lost. Bigger and bigger they waxed after a glass of whiskey. There was a comical feature of these fishing stories as told over the dinner table; Sir William got hold of every available spoon and fork to map out the plan of the struggle with Leviathan. We had a starched London butler, Mr. Cox, a man excelling in the setting-up of cocked-hat table napkins, immaculate silver and precision of cutlery. Behold Mr. Cox hovering in decorous rage while Sir William meanders tablespoons all over the damask ... an ever rising agony ... 'I even turned the fish' (behind the soup tureen more silver forks) 'but – he gave a tremend-i-ous wallop ...' The salmon parts from the hook, and Mr. Cox sweeps up the spoons and forks and rearranges the dinner table."

iii

Back in Bolton Gardens after these summer-long escapes, in a shadowy quiet that was almost unbroken now that Bertram was gone, Beatrix settled down to pursue the discoveries that they had made together. She drew and painted the pressed flowers that they had brought home in blotting paper; studied the skeletons of field-mice; reared a family of snails in a plant-pot, and kept a day to day record of their lives. And soon there was a pair of mice concealed in a box, and fed on milk and cracker crumbs after supper; and a rabbit which was supposed to live in a hutch in the back garden but which was generally stretched in civilized ease on the hearthrug, blinking at the fire; and bats, which hung upside-down in a parrot cage, and came zig-zagging across the room at dusk and settled on her fingers; and a hedgehog called Tiggy who drank out of a doll's tea-cup and eventually sickened, and was buried with dreadful tears in the back garden.

The time slipped away in deep absorption. Miss Hammond had come to the end of her educational resources, and retired. A visiting governess came for French, and one for German; but apart from the hours she spent with these her silent girlhood was passed without companions. She was growing up, and even when she put up her hair, and began to wear long dresses with a bustle, and on Sundays a gold watch and chain, nobody appears to have taken any notice. She was not taken for those regular two o'clock drives in the brougham, and no friends were asked to tea. The solitary life in the schoolroom went on as before. Her shyness deepened, and the contrast between her appearance and behaviour became noticeable: her silence, her resolute refusals to join in anything approaching youthful gaieties were so perplexingly belied by the timid and engaging glance, the air of slightly scared friendliness and anxiety to please, the readiness to smile and watch – even though nothing would induce her to come out of her corner. What in fact had happened was that the sociability of a naturally candid and affectionate nature had been driven inward by solitude; she had lost what childish confidence she once possessed, and as her growing-up was still unrecognized, there was nothing to take its place. She is remembered as unusually silent and old-fashioned, sitting against the wall whenever there was a dance for her cousins, refusing to dance or be introduced to anybody. She never stayed long: after an hour or two the chair in the corner would be empty, and Beatrix would have been called for by the Potters' coachman. She never went anywhere alone, except sometimes to the Natural History Museum at South Kensington, which was within a few minutes' walk of Bolton Gardens, and where she used to spend long mornings with her sketchbook, drawing stuffed animals and bones. Otherwise the coachman or a maid accompanied her, and shepherded her home.

The only breaks in the long monotony of growing up (if breaks they could be called) were the visits to relations which the Potters paid and the holidays they took – to Scotland, to the Lakes, to Camfield Place ("the place I love best in the world"), to aunts at Putney, to Hastings for Easter, to Sidmouth, to an uncle in Wales – always in the same rigid pattern . . . furnished houses . . . select lodgings . . . quiet hotels . . . the barouche . . . the promenade. The only change that we see, now that she has ceased to be merely Beatrix and has become Miss Potter, is that her luggage has become a little odd, is on the way to being eccentric. Beside the long serge skirts, the sensible boots, the practical umbrella, there stands on the station platform as often as not a travelling rabbit hutch – most useful on return journeys, when the rabbit can be accommodated under one's arm, and the hutch used for books, goloshes, sea-shells and other holiday accretions. "Now I am packing up for another journey on Tuesday and wondering how everything was stuffed in when we came. The rabbit hutch is a great resource upon such occasions, it is surprising what it will hold." Sometimes, on visits to relations, her companions travel unseen. "Hunca Munca is very discontented in the small old box; I am also accompanied by Mrs. Tiggy – carefully concealed; my aunt cannot endure animals." "I have got my hedgehog here with me too; she enjoys going by train, she is always very hungry when she is on a journey. I carry her in a little basket."

Soon Bertram has adopted her habit of travelling with a menagerie; he has bought a Barbary falcon, "so tame that it is quite silly. It climbs up his clothes and sits on his head, steals off his plate, and has broken two tea cups and burnt one of its wings with warming itself on the fender." Then an owl; "my brother has taken the owl to Scotland with him. I am rather glad because it makes a noise." The owl is said to be a great nuisance, because "it hoots all night. If he has a dead mouse he bites its head off and then shouts as loud as he can." Travelling to and from Scotland, the Lakes, the seaside, becomes summer by summer more complicated. Bertram "has gone away to Scotland; he had a jackdaw and a dog as well – such a many parcels. I shall have still more: a rabbit, a large family of snails, and eleven minnows! I shall have to squirt air into the bottle to keep the minnows alive. I bought two squirts for fear one might break on the journey..." She had made friends with rabbits and hedgehogs, mice and minnows, as a prisoner in solitary confinement will befriend a mouse.

CHAPTER
THREE

Peter Rabbit

i

Brother and sister were now grown up. Bertram had finished his last year at Charterhouse, Beatrix was in her early twenties. The time had come for the boy to consider a career (for the girl, of course, the question did not arise); and without delay he chose to be an artist.

Mr. and Mrs. Potter offered no opposition to his plan; he would continue to live at home, and would accompany them, with canvases, on their summer holidays. There was fortunately no suggestion of a separate studio, models, Paris, or anything of that sort; his tastes lay in the direction of Scottish scenery and mist, to which nobody could possibly take objection. Soon we hear that "my brother catches fish when it rains and paints a picture on fine days"; "my brother has painted a very large picture in Scotland, a moor and hills and fir trees. He has been very much vexed with the windy weather; it is not easy to carry a large picture up a hill in a high wind; I expect he will be blown away some day like a big kite."

Painting and pictures were deeply interesting to the whole family, with the possible exception of Mrs. Potter. Mr. Potter regularly attended exhibitions at the Royal

Academy – "a great resource," Beatrix privately considered, "for people of our station" – and occasionally she
was permitted to accompany him. Their progress round
the galleries must have been slow, for she early developed
the habit of making notes in her catalogue and writing her
personal criticism of the pictures. "Flat, sentimental and
unpleasant colour," she wrote at sixteen, disliking a Marcus
Stone. And of another artist, more kindly, "Large and
striking picture, painting good and may improve. Some of
perspective in woodwork doubtful." Even Michelangelo,
since her diary was private, did not escape. "Went upstairs
for a few minutes, looked at the old Italian pictures. No
one will read this. I say fearlessly that the Michelangelo
is hideous and badly drawn; I wouldn't give tuppence for
it except as a curiosity." Then, as time goes on, her
comments become more technical. "Did Reynolds paint
the animals himself, if he did not paint the drapery in his
portraits? I do not think they are all painted by the same
hand. Most of them are bad, and the preference for
long-haired dogs seems to suggest timidness about their
drawing." The pre-Raphaelites are at fault in having all
parts of a picture in focus at once. The face in one of
Millais' portraits has "several holes in it where the other
coats of paint had not taken." Then, "What are the
canvases primed with? What is drying oil?" Poor Holman
Hunt deserves sympathy over his *Flight into Egypt*. "He
has been working on the subject seven years. The first was
only on calico because he had no canvas, and broke down
under the weight of the paint." The problems of painting,
evidently, were endless; moving from room to room, from
canvas to canvas, she pondered on technicalities and theories. "Nature, with the exception of water and air, is
made of colour. There is no such thing as its absence . . .

What we call the highest and the lowest in nature are both equally perfect. A willow bush is as beautiful as the human form divine."

Encouraged by her brother's example, though never for a moment considering herself on his level, Beatrix gave more and more time to drawing and water-colours, evolving for herself, in her solitary fashion, almost a student's life of regular hours at the Victoria and Albert and South Kensington museums, where she drew embroideries, insects, fossils. Where Bertram's tastes were for the large and vague, for moorlands, sunsets, misty glens and stags, all painted on a formidable scale, hers were for the precise and the minute, for the fine details of a plant, mosses under the microscope, the fabric of a mouse's nest, the eye of a squirrel. She drew like a naturalist – no leaf too modest, no twig too small for her attention. Long hours were spent with her eye to Bertram's microscope, drawing the spores of mould with their thread-like growth, or in museums leaning with sketchbook and pencil over the fossil cases. She became obsessed with the study of geology, and since she was now allowed to use an old camera of her father's which he had decided was too heavy, holidays were enlivened by photographic expeditions (accompanied by Mr. Potter or the coachman) on which she photographed rocks and quarries and collected her own fossils. The journal at this point is suddenly full of boulders and screes and speculations about strata – still in cipher, as though the subject, like everything else that interested her, must be kept secret – and the taste for scientific matters, which she had shared with Bertram in the days when they had filled their bone-cupboards, developed into a serious pursuit which transformed the summers. Even more absorbing than coloured microscopic forests or the spirals of vanished shells revealed in stone were the bewildering funguses to be found every autumn, whether they went to Scotland or the Lakes. Some were slender and fairylike, coloured like amethysts and curiously smoky; others lay scattered like birds' eggs through the fir plantations. Some resembled studs of ruby set in the short grass, others grew like golden coral on the rubbish heap in the shrubbery, a few clung to the potting shed like barnacles. There were no two alike. Soon we hear "I have been drawing funguses very hard; I think some day they will be put in a book, but it will be a dull one to read. We have had one little fungus like red holly berries – it had only been found once before in Scotland . . ."

We detect a note of genuine excitement in the note-books. "Was overtaken with funguses, especially *Hygrophorus*. Found a lovely pink one. They begin to come in crowds, exasperating to leave." And then, as the days fly past, "I found upwards of twenty sorts in a few minutes . . . and joy of joys, the spiky *Gomphidius glutinosus*, a round, slimy, purple head among the moss, which I took up carefully with my old cheese-knife, and turning over saw the slimy veil. There is extreme complacency in finding a totally new species for the first time." The collecting and drawing of specimens went on and on until mid-October, when she could scarcely tear herself away. "I was very sorry indeed to come away, with a feeling of not having half worked through the district, but I have done a good summer's work."

It really seemed, when once she was back in London, that the months she had spent on her funguses might at last bear fruit. The idea of illustrating a book on the subject seriously took hold of her. Over a number of years she had made hundreds of beautifully exact drawings, with minute patience identifying and classifying specimens, dissecting, comparing varieties and checking details at the Natural History Museum. (This last was a rather unnerving business, for "at the Natural History Museum the clerks seem to be all gentlemen and one must not speak to them. If people are forward," she decided, "I can manage them, but if they take the line of being shocked it is perfectly awful to a shy person.")

Help, however, came unexpectedly in 1896 in the person of her uncle, Sir Henry Roscoe, who, being himself a chemist of some distinction (he had been knighted in 1884 for his services to science) was more sympathetic than her parents to this cherished project. In a "sudden fit of kindness" he proposed taking her to Kew, and this, an event almost tremulously recorded, was the first of a series of meetings with the Director of the Royal Botanic Gardens and other august botanists. The question of whether she would be allowed to go with her "discreet uncle" was never certain: on one occasion, being "afraid of being stopped from going", she "escaped out of the house soon after eight and walked up and down Bramham Gardens to the puzzlement of housemaids" until Uncle Harry emerged to take her to the train.

The botanical experts at the Herbarium were sceptical. "I am exclusively tropical," the Assistant Director told her, waving aside her portfolios of water-colours. They were passed on to another pontiff, "a slim, timid-looking old gentleman with a large, thin book under his arm, and an appearance of having been dried in blotting-paper under a press," and eventually into the presence of the Director himself, an intimidating person with "a dry cynical manner, puffing a cigarette, but wide awake and boastful." He glanced at the drawings, appeared to be surprised at what he saw, and conversed with Uncle Harry about politics. "He did not address me again, which I mention not with resentment, for I was getting dreadfully tired, but I had once or twice an amusing feeling of being regarded as young."

The trouble was, as soon unmistakeably appeared, that an amateur was not quite welcome in these precincts. Not only were the water-colours, as the Director with evident pleasure pointed out, lacking the diagrammatic extension of detail necessary for scientific usefulness, but this unknown young woman had conducted independent experiments and developed theories. She even went so far as to have her own ideas about the propagation of the spores of moulds, and to offer a theory that lichens were actually dual organisms, funguses living in close association with algae. (In this, as it later turned out, she was perfectly right, though forestalled in her small discovery by a learned German.) The Assistant Director was sceptical, and said so. The Director, Mr. Thiselton-Dyer, after further visits had been paid to the Herbarium, wrote a letter to Sir Henry which was not only "stupid" (or so Uncle Harry considered it) but "rude". "Uncle Harry said he was a little rough-spoken and knew nothing about the subject . . . He would not show me his letter. I imagine it contained advice that I should be sent to school before I began to teach other people." Sir Henry was justifiably affronted, and "expressed animosity against the authorities at Kew". He would not, he could not, he insisted, let the matter rest. "Upon my word I was afraid the Director would have taken away my ticket." (She had been issued a reader's ticket to the Library.) "I fancy he may be something of a misogynist, *vide* the girls in the garden who are obliged to wear knickerbockers; but it is odious

41

to a shy person to be snubbed as conceited, especially when the shy person happened to be right, and under the temptation of sauciness."

The upshot of this "storm in a tea-kettle", as she considered it, was that Beatrix was egged on by her uncle to write a paper on the burning subject of the spores of moulds, which he went over minutely for corrections, and which was finally, at his suggestion, read before the Linnaean Society of London. Not, however, by its author; ladies were not allowed to attend meetings. This was something, certainly, but it was not much. The excitement of several years had ended in disappointment, and though Beatrix for a time continued in her passion for funguses – "I perceived a stout, elderly joiner removing quantities of dry rotten wood from the shop front of Slater the greengrocer. I had an eye on him all day, and went out after dark with a paper bag and a sixpence" – she knew now that it would lead nowhere. One by one, with reluctance, the treasured folios of water-colours were laid aside. Their tapes, it seemed, would after all be untied only for the interest of an occasional visitor; and who besides Bertram (and perhaps, at a pinch, Canon Rawnsley) could be expected to understand the beauties of fungus? For comfort, she turned to copying the nursery-rhyme pictures of Randolph Caldecott and making ingenious trick pictures of rabbit families for her cousins' nurseries.

These she thought of only as an amusement, the trick pictures and fantastic animal scenes which she painted to please herself and other people's children, and she sometimes regretted the more serious and grown-up work which had been abandoned; but even in this trivial occupation she had three sources of encouragement – her brother, the children on whom she bestowed her working models of furnished mouse-holes and rabbits' greengrocery shops, and Canon H. D. Rawnsley.

ii

Canon Rawnsley had been vicar of Wray, a parish on Lake Windermere, when Beatrix was twelve years old, and not many years after this Mr. Potter had discovered Wray Castle, a turreted essay in the Victorian baronial style, appropriately furnished and very much to his taste, which could be rented in the summer. He added it to the list of large houses, both in Scotland and the Lakes, which he occupied according to choice in the holiday months; and it was from here and other Lake District houses that Beatrix, in the years of growing up and in her twenties, came to know the lakes and fells, the scattered farms and lonely places of this poetic and beautiful part of the north country.

She and her parents also, in the course of their Wray Castle summer of 1882, came to know Canon Rawnsley; the acquaintance survived the Canon's removing from Wray to become vicar of Crosthwaite, near Keswick; and both Beatrix and her father delighted, for different reasons, in the invigorating company of this most charming of men. Mr. Potter found him interesting as an authority on the Lake Country, with already a number of published books to his credit; he was moreover ready to give advice on Mr. Potter's new hobby of collecting autographed letters of the Lake Poets, and to correspond with him freely on religious matters in a brisk and uninhibited style which, since there were very few people living who could decipher the

Canon's handwriting, provided almost a sporting interest for Mr. Potter. To Beatrix he was even more appealing, for in the warmth of his physical and mental vigour, which was prodigious, her shyness melted, and she made the stimulating discovery that it was possible for grown-up people to have enthusiasms.

The Canon had many, and was moreover always ready to give battle or bully a committee on behalf of any of them. He had become by common consent the champion of the Lakes, challenging and defying the builders of bungalows and the extenders of railways, tilting single-handed against all the dangers which already menaced this lovely and tripper-ridden district. When the Potters first encountered him he was crusading hotly for the formation of a National Trust to buy and preserve places of natural beauty and historic interest for the nation – an ambition which he achieved in 1895, together with Miss Octavia Hill and Sir Robert Hunter. These three working together were an ideal combination for the purpose. Octavia Hill, well known as a sincere philanthropist, was the right figure to engage public sympathy; Sir Robert Hunter gave legal knowledge and his natural ingenuity to the cause; Canon Rawnsley was the dynamo. And from the foundation of the Trust, the Canon became more than ever jovially formidable in the north. He waged war on jerry-builders, like a scorpion he skirmished round the demolishers of ancient bridges, he spiked the guns of expanding tramway companies. He was prepared to travel anywhere and tackle anybody, and the ring of his energetic boots and the very shadow of his beard struck terror into council meetings and committees.

All this was very interesting to Beatrix, who sympathized with his views and admired his pugnacity; and the Canon had other endearing qualities which drew her to him. He was an amateur naturalist, like herself, and in his boyhood had skinned and stuffed and anatomized to the very limits of endurance. He was an antiquarian, too, as well as a lover of nature, and liked nothing better than to raise a fund to erect a stone to commemorate something or somebody that everyone else had forgotten; unless, perhaps, it were to walk his friends all night over the fells to reach a particular peak in time for a special sunrise, which he would contemplate with a picnic basket and describe afterwards in a sonnet. He wrote verses on any and every occasion, sometimes felicitously, sometimes in a vein of romping rectory humour, and always without the least shadow of self-consciousness. He published his poems in book form and he sent them to the newspapers, without misgiving as without pretentiousness, always regarding them (as indeed they were simply) as an agreeable way of saying this or that, and an innocent diversion. One cannot complete the catalogue of his achievements and activities without adding that he was an ardent traveller, the author of more than a score of books, a Canon of Carlisle, a friend of Tennyson, a campaigner against objectionable postcards and a great organizer of bonfires. It is worth mentioning that on the night of Queen Victoria's jubilee in 1887 no fewer than a hundred and forty-eight of Canon Rawnsley's bonfires could be seen from the top of Skiddaw.

This lively and engaging clergyman was the first man of letters, the first published author whom Beatrix had encountered; he had taken a great interest in her funguses and had encouraged her painting (even those fantasies which she invented for children at Christmas, and which her elderly aunts at Putney considered "silly"); so that it was to him that she naturally turned for advice when the idea occurred to her, as it did in her middle thirties, that she might privately venture on a modest little children's book, *The Tale of Peter Rabbit.*

iii

Her middle thirties ... Then what had happened in the intervening years, since she first put up her hair, wore a gold watch and chain on Sundays, and took to driving about (with the coachman) in a pony carriage? This is a question which until recently – until 1958, to be precise – appeared to have no answer. There was a gap of fifteen years in Beatrix Potter's life, from her middle teens until she was close on thirty, of which nobody, not even her one-time governesses or her surviving cousins, could remember anything. Yet, unknown to everyone, the journal begun in childhood had gone on and on, and had lain undiscovered in a drawer at Castle Cottage, Sawrey, until the year 1952, when Mrs. Stephanie Duke, the first cousin once removed who had inherited the house, and who had been the child to whom *The Tale of Mr. Jeremy Fisher* had been dedicated, came upon the bundle in the attic. She could make nothing of it. It contained a "most extraordinary collection of papers ... a large bundle of loose sheets and exercise books written in cipher-writing which we can make nothing of ..." This was the 200,000 word record which was eventually decoded and transcribed by Mr. Leslie Linder and published in 1966, the centenary of her birth, as *The Journal of Beatrix Potter.*

To unravel this extraordinary story we must go forward from the Bolton Garden days to 1952, when Mr. Linder, an engineer who in middle life had made a hobby of collecting Beatrix Potter's works, her paintings, drawings, photographs and anything else that had any relevance to her, paid one of his visits to Sawrey and learned from Mrs. Duke of the existence of the code-writings, which by this time had been deposited at Hill Top in the care of the National Trust. (Sawrey, as we shall see presently, was the Lancashire village where Beatrix Potter bought her first small freehold farm, and where she lived, in Castle Cottage, from her marriage in 1913 until her death.)

Mr. Linder lost no time in examining the papers, but they defeated him. He "could find no clue to the cipher-symbols, apart from the fact that some of them looked like ordinary letters of the alphabet, also the figure 3 appeared very frequently." (Her code, as he later discovered, for "the".) "There was, however, an indication of the period covered, since the figures '83, '84 etc., had been marked in the top right-hand corner of some of the sheets ... Also, at the beginning of some of the exercise books, Beatrix Potter had put the year, 1892, 1893 etc."

He was allowed to take specimen sheets home with him for study, and for four years devoted his spare time to them, still without success. Help was sought from a professional code-breaker, with no better result. It began to look as though the mysterious papers – so neat, so deliberately private and minutely written – would keep their secret. Mr. Linder decided to return them. And then, "On the evening of Easter Monday, 1958, I remember thinking to myself, I will have one *last* attempt at solving this code-writing, more to pass the time than with any anticipation of success. I selected a sheet at random, and then, quite by chance, noticed a line near the bottom of the page which contained the Roman numerals XVI and the year

1793. Was this a clue – could something of consequence have happened to a Pope bearing the numerals XVI, or to King Louis XVI in the year 1793? I consulted a *Dictionary of Dates* without success, and then ... the index to the *Children's Encyclopaedia*, where I read, 'Louis XVI, French King; born Versailles 1754; guillotined Paris 1793.' Here at last was a possible clue!"

The clue was valid. The word which followed the date contained an X, and he made the obvious guess that it might be "executed". Again he was fortunate, and "with the help of these assumed symbols, other words were deciphered, and by midnight on that memorable Easter Monday practically the whole of Beatrix Potter's code alphabet had been solved".

The complete deciphering took him another five years, for apart from the difficulties of the code, the script-writings themselves, like the stitches in the Tailor of Gloucester's buttonholes, were "so small – *so* small – they looked as though they had been made by little mice". Some of the pages had been written in pencil, and then inked over. Some were mere scraps and fragments, unrelated to the rest. The code originals of those early pages of transcription which her cousin Mrs. Clark of Ulva had carefully kept, were never found at all. But at last the gigantic task was finished – more than 200,000 words of a private record which Beatrix Potter never dreamed that anyone but herself would ever read – and the curious gap in her life was filled at last.

Why, one finally wonders, had she concealed it? For nothing emerges more clearly, as we turn the pages of the published journal, than that there was nothing, by ordinary standards, to conceal. No hidden self-communings, no secret fantasy, even singularly few complaints. She seems to have embarked on this labour of many years almost in spite of herself, driven by a restless urge to use her faculties, to stretch her mind, to let nothing of significance escape, to create *something*. And perhaps after reading Fanny Burney's diary, which she admired, and because she had been early impressed by the information that Pepys's diary had been written in private shorthand, she began to experiment; and finding privacy delightful in itself, and the code a perfect defence against interference, perfected her cipher until she could write it as rapidly as she wrote everything. "No-one will read this", she wrote decisively. If the breaking of the code has caused her to turn in her grave, at least the difficulty of elucidating it must have given her some ironical satisfaction.

For all its length, it is a curiously impersonal document. She is obsessed with the past, recording scraps of her mother's or her grandmother's reminiscences, however trivial, so that they shall not be forgotten. Her visit to a silversmith's with her grandmother, or to the Royal Academy with Papa (for Mr. Potter was interested in painting, and even drew quite well before he took up photography) are recounted with painstaking minuteness. Page after page, meticulous detail after detail, the strangely unchildish diary gets into its stride. The newspapers are diligently read, Papa's testy comments silently attended to. (It is an item culled from a newspaper, perhaps read aloud and commented on by Mr. Potter, which provides the clue by which Mr. Linder profited. "An old woman was buried at Paris last Saturday aged 107, who was present at the execution of Louis XVI in 1793.") Scraps of information are hoarded and set down. ("The proper way to clean unpolished slate chimney-pieces is to wash them with milk ... The nursemaids in Berlin may only wheel perambulators in their own streets, and have always to have a licence.")

But here and there, as we proceed, there are indications of dismay at the loss of childhood; the outwardly stolid young person that she had become in her teens realized, with a sense of shock, that it was over, and that in spite of its monotony and "the tyranny of a cross old nurse" it had been a happy time. She dreads going back to Dalguise for the holidays, the house on the River Tay where, at five years old, she had first discovered the delights of the countryside. "I am afraid there is a chance of going back to Dalguise. I feel an extraordinary dislike to this idea, a childish dislike, but the memory of that home is the only bit of childhood I have left ... The place is changed now, and many familiar faces are gone, but the greatest change is in myself. I was a child then, I had no idea what the world would be like ... It has been a terrible time since, and the future is dark and uncertain; let me keep the past." It was at Dalguise, as a very small child, that she had had a loving friendship with Mr. Gaskell, who in old age had lost none of his wisdom and gentle charm. When she was eight she had knitted him a comforter for Christmas, and still had his letter of thanks, assuring her that "Big as I am I know I could not have done it one-tenth as well." Now she was seventeen, and Mr. Gaskell was dead. Her memory of him was so alive that she had only to shut her eyes to escape into the past. "Oh how plainly I see it again. He is sitting comfortably in the warm sunshine on the doorstep at Dalguise, in his grey coat and old felt hat. The newspaper lies on his knees, suddenly he looks up with his gentle smile. There are sounds of pounding footsteps. The blue-bottles whizz off the path. A little girl in a print frock and striped stockings bounds to his side and offers

50

him a bunch of meadowsweet. He just says, 'Thank you, dear,' and puts his arm round her . . . Shall I really never see him again? It is all gone, and he is resting quietly with our fathers. I have begun the dark journey of life. Will it go on as darkly as it has begun?"

For more than a year now, from the time when she had turned sixteen, she had been uneasily aware that childhood was gone for ever, and she mistrusted what little she had seen of the grown-up world. "Old year going fast," she wrote at the end of 1882, five months after her sixteenth birthday. "It's not been one to forget, it has been the comer – the wicket-gate. I'm glad I've been helped past it." And fourteen years later, when she was past thirty, she was still reverting in code to those halcyon years, acknowledging their private happiness and all that she owed them. "What heaven can be more real than to retain the spirit-world of childhood, tempered and balanced by knowledge and common-sense, to fear no longer the terror that flieth by night, yet to feel truly and understand a little, a very little, of the story of life."

This concern for words and passion for writing which was so large a part of her secret life during adolescence was matched, even superseded, by the passion for drawing. Towards this her parents seem to have shown some sympathy, for at twelve she began to have serious drawing lessons, which continued with a certain Miss Cameron until she was seventeen. "I have great reason to be grateful to her, though we were not on particularly good terms for the last good while. I have learnt from her free-hand, model, geometry, perspective and a little water-colour flower painting." Evidently she was not a docile pupil, having definite ideas of her own from the beginning. Miss Cameron was succeeded by "Mrs. A." and a short course of figure-drawing and oils. ("Can have no more because Mrs. A's charge is high.") "Of course," she confided to her journal, "I shall paint just as I like when not with her ... I am convinced it lies chiefly with oneself." The lessons were not a success. "I don't much like it, which is disappointing. Wish it did not cost so much ... It is tiresome, when you do get some lessons, to be taught in a way you dislike and to have to swallow your feelings out of considerations at home ... I do wish these drawing lessons were over so that I could have some peace and sleep of nights."

The lessons came to an end at last, and she could indulge her passion for drawing without interference. "It is all the same, drawing, painting, modelling, the irresistible desire to copy any beautiful object which strikes the eye. Why cannot one be content to look at it? I cannot rest, I *must* draw, however poor the result, and when I have a bad time come over me it is a stronger desire than ever, and settles on the queerest thing, worse than queer sometimes. Last time, in the middle of September, I caught myself in the back yard making a careful and admiring copy of the swill bucket, and the laugh it gave me brought me round."

The "bad times" obliquely referred to were recurring depressions. She was increasingly lonely, suffered from faintness and rheumatic pains, was always tired. "How much I have to be thankful for, but these odious fits of low spirits would spoil any life." Even going to exhibitions with Papa exhausted her, however much she liked the paintings, or was amused by the crowd. "How is it that these high-heeled ladies who dine out, paint and pinch their waists to deformity, can racket about all day long, while I who sleep o'nights, can turn in my stays, and dislike sweets and dinners, am so tired towards the end of the afternoon that I can scarcely keep my feet?" The only thing that did not tire her was painting; and for this she must be left alone, and given time. "There's no word about my painting just now," she wrote, having returned to London after yet another family excursion, "and I don't want any except for more time. I don't want lessons, I want practice. I hope it is not pride that makes me so stiff against teaching, but a bad or indifferent teacher is worse than none. It cannot be taught." She worked doggedly on in the privacy of the schoolroom, undisturbed now even by the last of the governesses, for Miss Carter had ceased her lessons when Beatrix turned eighteen. In the company of a tame rabbit or two, or a lizard in a cardboard box, the room was marvellously quiet. She was free to draw whatever caught her attention – the bones that she and Bertram had collected during many holidays, and which now filled several dusty cupboards; the tortoise wandering on the hearthrug; the tall Wellington chest where she kept her drawings and specimens; even the flat-iron which was a relic of nursery days and still, with other odds and ends, occupied the chimneypiece. The most trivial thing was absorbing when one began to draw it, and she dreaded being fetched away because elderly cousins had come to tea, or to go calling with Mama. For all its loneliness, this busy solitude was the best, indeed the only defence against depression. "Oh life," she wrote at the end of 1885, "wearisome, disappointing, and yet in many shades so sweet, I wonder why one is so unwilling to let go this old year? – not because it has been joyful, but because I fear its successors – I am terribly afraid of the future." In another seven months she would be twenty.

The recurring malaise reached a crisis during these

gloomy months, and she fell ill with rheumatic fever. How long the illness lasted we do not know; it was not a theme on which she cared to be expansive. But it left her very weak, and convalescence was slow. She could not draw, and for six months added nothing to the journal. "Part of the time I was too ill, and since then the laziness and unsettledness consequent on weakness have so demoralised me, that I have persevered in nothing for more than a week at a time except toothache." Her hair had fallen out in alarming quantities, and had finally been cropped as short as Bertram's to save what remained. "Had my few remaining locks clipped short at Douglas's. Draughty. My hair nearly all came off since I was ill. Now that the sheep is shorn I can say without pride that I have seldom seen a more beautiful head of hair than mine. Last summer it was very thick and within about four inches of my knees, being more than a yard long." The symptoms of rheumatic fever recurred at intervals for about two years, sometimes so severely that she "could not be turned in bed without screaming", but at length her health improved and she began to go about again, beset more than ever by the admonitions of her parents, since it was suspected that the illness had permanently damaged her heart.

Once she was well, and could travel, the Potter holidays resumed their inexorable round. A month in the spring, three months in the summer, the household was packed up and transferred to seaside lodgings (where sometimes there were bugs), or to the various country houses to which the carriage and horses followed by goods-train, and where Mr. and Mrs. Potter were inevitably displeased with the arrangements. "It is somewhat trying," Beatrix wrote in cipher in a rare moment of exasperation, "to pass a season of enjoyment in the company of persons who are constantly on the outlook for matters of complaint."

London as always, apart from the art galleries and the museums, remained largely unknown territory. Her own ignorance of it, on the rare occasions when the Potter carriage ventured beyond the confines of South Kensington, struck her as absurd. "I thought the drive there was the most interesting part of the affair," she wrote after the unaccustomed treat of being taken to the theatre to see *The Private Secretary*. "Extraordinary to state, it was the first time in my life that I had been past the Horse Guards, Admiralty and Whitehall, or seen the Strand and the Monument." And even ten years later, when at twenty-nine she accompanied her father to an exhibition of relics in the church of All Hallows, Barking, the astonishment persisted. "It was the first City church I have been in, which is a little hard considering I have lived nearly thirty years in London, and studied many ancient works of topography from Stow downwards."

It was the boredom of doing nothing that was so intolerable. She filled her days with every conceivable activity within her reach; all was comparatively well so long as she could pursue her "work" in peace. The thirst for work itself was like a fever; drawing, painting, reading were not enough; even the long hours devoted to the codewriting – and the journal by now had assumed gargantuan proportions – left wakeful hours which she must somehow justify. Alone in her room, often in bed at night or in the early morning, she set about learning the plays of Shakespeare by heart, testing and training her always extraordinary memory. "I know *Richard III* right through," she noted in 1894, "*Henry VIth* four fifths, *Richard II* except three pages, *King John* four acts, a good half the *Midsummer Night's Dream* and *The Tempest*, half way through *The Merchant of Venice* and *Henry VIII* . . . I learnt six more or less in a year. Never felt the least strained or should not have done it." Indeed, there was a sense of peace and enjoyment in these quiet sessions of memorizing the plays, and sometimes she was not alone. "I . . . learned four acts of *Henry VIII* and ought to have learned all, but I can say this for my diligence, that every line was learnt in bed. The 4th Act is associated with the company of a robin who came in at daylight attracted by sleepy flies, and sat on the curtain-pole or the wardrobe, bold and black-eyed. He only once sang. The swallows used to fly round the next room. Mice were also an amusement and extremely tame, picking up crumbs from the table." She recited the plays to herself interminably, entering good or bad marks on a chart to record progress.

There were records kept of another kind as well, illustrated letters which were more like dreams than communications, water-colours of rabbits or lizards which were precise enough, yet had a touch of fantasy, scribblings and verses which only she could identify. The shallow drawers of the Wellington chest were full of such beginnings, of designs that look like ideas for Christmas cards and calendars, of scraps of drawings and verses and picture-letters, and eventually a loose-leaf booklet which had ceased to be a secret, since it had actually been published.

This booklet, so small and cheap that it has become as scarce and difficult to trace as a forgotten almanac, is a curiosity because it seems to have been Beatrix Potter's first appearance as an illustrator – not of her own work, but of some doggerel verses by Frederic E. Weatherly. It is not bound like a book; its seven gilt-edged pages and stiff paper cover are held together by a pink silk cord after the manner of a Christmas card, and it was published by the firm of Hildesheimer and Faulkner and sold for fourpence-halfpenny. *A Happy Pair* has, in fact, little to distinguish it from the general run of children's illustrated booklets which, under the imprint of various English publishers, were printed in Germany at this period for the Christmas market, together with scraps and transfers and greetings cards, the stock-in-trade of German colour-lithography; nothing, that is, beyond a certain charm in the illustrations (which are all of rabbits), and the initials "H.B.P." in the corner of each picture. Beatrix Potter's name nowhere appears, and the rabbit pictures, though in the same *genre* as the animal fantasies which she drew so readily, are not, at first glance, easy to identify as hers. There is a touch of caricature, and something of the scrapbook scrap about them, which is unfamiliar; they lack the poetic truth and innocence of her best work. This slight unfamiliarity of the style has probably two origins – the German colour-lithograph process of printing the water-colours, which always tends to give a stereotyped and transfer-like appearance, and Beatrix Potter's own admiration for the work of Randolph Caldecott, some of whose nursery rhyme pictures hung on the walls of her room at Bolton Gardens. "I did try to copy Caldecott," she wrote in old age, remembering the traditions that had influenced her, "but I agree . . . that I did *not* achieve much resemblance." The doggerel verses accompanying the little pictures are banal to a degree, and in turning the pages we begin to wonder what in the world could have brought Beatrix Potter and Frederic Weatherly together, and even whether "H.B.P." were Helen Beatrix Potter after all, and not some unknown illustrator. But the last picture but one removes all doubt. It is of a rabbit waiting on a railway platform, with his umbrella, carpet bag and labelled boxes, and the verse accompanying it is called *Benjamin Bunny*.

> "My name's Mister Benjamin Bunny,
> And I travel about without money,
> There are lots I could name,
> Do precisely the same,
> It's convenient, but certainly funny!"

Frederic Weatherly, then, must have known Miss Potter, and her habit of taking pet rabbits about on her journeys. He had met her, most probably, through the publishers themselves, for in that year, 1890, Beatrix had sent them some sketches of "that charming rascal Benjamin Bouncer, our tame Jack Hare" as suggestions for Christmas cards, and Mr. Faulkner had responded by saying that "he thought we should be able to do business." They had already done business with Mr. Weatherly, a prolific versifier. He was, in fact, a remarkably energetic barrister who for many years conducted a heavy legal practice from Bristol and wrote more than three thousand popular songs (*Roses of Picardy* is the best known) in his spare time, composing in trains and while eating his meals in provincial hotels on circuit. There are no other clues; the booklet is undated, but from the fact that Faulkner was publishing apart from Hildesheimer by 1893 one would guess that *A Happy Pair* had appeared before that date, and it was probably an 1890 Christmas publication.

The collaboration did not, apparently, give Miss Potter much satisfaction, for the experiment seems never to have been repeated, and she refused in 1904, when five of her own books for children had already been published, to illustrate a story by another writer. "I do not think I can undertake the illustrations," she wrote to her publishers, Frederick Warne & Co. "With regard to illustrating other people's books, I have a strong feeling that every outside book which I did, would prevent me from finishing one of my own. I enjoy inventing stories – any number – but I draw so slowly and laboriously that there are sure to be favourites of my own left undone at the end of my working lifetime, whether short or long. Illustrators soon begin to go downhill; I will stick to doing as many as I can of my own books." And in 1942, the year before her death, when the editor of *The Horn Book* (an American magazine concerned with publications for children) wrote to ask if she had ever illustrated any books beside her own, she replied, "No – never illustrated any for another author." So perhaps, by the time she was seventy-six, she had forgotten *A Happy Pair* and Mr. Weatherly.

iv

The illustrated letters, those other relics from this same period, are in a different category. Some of them, now, are more than half a century old, and they are fragile with handling. They are quite unlike the letters which people usually keep, being not in the least like the letters that are usually written. They are written to children.

In order to unearth the beginnings of this correspondence we must go back to about the year 1883, when Beatrix Potter was seventeen. At that time she had a visiting governess for French, and somebody had recommended a governess for German. Choice fell on Miss Annie Carter, a young woman very little older than Beatrix herself, sweet-natured, pleasant mannered, and – compared with Beatrix – splendidly emancipated. Miss Carter had gone to Germany as a student and knew the meaning of "abroad"; she spoke German fluently and was not afraid to travel; most curious and interesting of all, she was self-supporting. The German lessons were a fair success and Beatrix enjoyed them; but they did not last long. Miss Carter rounded off her adventures by falling in love and marrying on very little money, and then going to live at Wandsworth and starting to produce a charming and numerous family.

Beatrix had been fond of Miss Carter, and now that she had become Mrs. Moore the interest deepened. Almost every year there was a new baby to be visited and considered, and Beatrix would drive to Wandsworth with presents of shawls and long-clothes in her pony carriage. And it was not only the newest baby that was interesting; as each in turn emerged from infancy there was a still keener pleasure in watching their explorations into the world of first impressions and sensations. She remembered exactly what it had been like to be five years old; in some respects the freshness had never faded. Animals, for instance, had never lost their startling character and individuality, which she had first perceived among the bracken fronds more than twenty years ago. Even the white ducks at Putney Park, where her aunts lived, seemed still to pause and consider her with the same surprise, to come to the same conclusions, as when she had worn a pinafore. And Noël, the first of the Moore children, knew exactly what she meant. By the time he was running about there was perfect accord and sharing of interests between them.

It was very odd, but Miss Potter, the dowdily dressed

lady with the bright blue eyes, who always came in a pony carriage with a coachman, knew exactly what interested children, and was able to do magic things with paint-brush and pencil. Without, moreover, showing any trace of sentimental indulgence, or of a fond grown-up's descent to a childish level. No, she told stories and drew pictures on terms of perfect equality, and as though to please herself. She was remembering something; stepping back, with Noël's help, into a magic world which was still – oh, incomparably – the best she knew, and to which she often in imagination still returned. The child in her had not been superseded or outgrown, and the bright areas of first discovery and experience were still real to her, and alive with an innocent outdoor freshness, green secret oases in the desert of being grown-up. (Fifty years later, looking back, she was to write, "I have just made stories to please myself, because I never grew up," and there is truth, of a limited kind, in this assertion. But it would have been truer still to say, "because the child in me lived on, concealed, until I was fifty." There was no suggestion, ever, of Peter Pan; the woman developed and matured, the character deepened and set until it had acquired a salty Crompton tang and masculine flavour. But the child, with her morning vision and spark of genius, lived on, and the woman was well into middle-age before she vanished entirely.)

When he was five years old, Noël fell ill; it was a long illness, lasting many months; and Miss Potter, who was still gravitationally committed to the Potter orbit according to the seasons, and who therefore could not come to Wandsworth very often, began to write him letters. They were letters full of her own doings, and the doings of her rabbit, Peter. They were also full of tiny and exquisite pictures. Sometimes, when things were duller than usual and there was really no news, they simply told a story.

Eastwood, Dunkeld
Sep 4th, 93

My dear Noël,
    I don't know what to write to you, so I shall tell you a story about four little rabbits, whose names were Flopsy, Mopsy, Cottontail and Peter.
    They lived with their Mother in a sand bank under the root of a big fir tree.
    "Now, my dears," said old Mrs. Bunny, "you may go into the field or down the lane, but don't go into Mr. McGregor's garden . . ."

The letter turns over, page after yellowed page. Here is Peter Rabbit among the lettuces, here Mr. McGregor pursuing with his rake; and the words, read and chanted over and over again in the nurseries of two generations, fall on the mind's ear like an incantation.
    There is more to come. In this bundle of letters scattered on the table and in these few shabby exercise books lie the first hints and outlines, the first spontaneous bubblings-up of fancy which later were to give us the stories and characters we should love all our lives. Some were written to Noël, some to his brother and sisters, some to other children, and there is scarcely one that does not contain a suggestion of the little masterpieces to come. "My dear Eric, Once upon a time there was a frog called Mr. Jeremy Fisher, and he lived in a little house on the bank of a river . . . One morning Mr. Fisher looked out and saw drops of rain . . ."

"There is a lady who lives on an island in the lake who told me some curious things about animals swimming. She had a cat which she did not want, so she gave it to someone in Keswick, but a week afterwards it came back into her house, dripping wet! Also when her nuts are ripe, squirrels appear on the island, but she has not seen them coming. There is an American story that squirrels go down the river on little rafts, using their tails for sails, but I think the Keswick squirrels must swim."

"Hunca Munca is very much alive; she was caught in a mouse-trap two years ago, and now she is so tame she will sit on my finger. She lives in a cage with another mouse called Appley Dapply."

"I was looking at a ship called the *Pearl of Falmouth* which was being mended ... when I heard something grunt. I went up a bank where I could see on to the deck, and there was a white pig with a curly tail walking about. It is a ship that goes to Newfoundland, and the sailors always take a pig. I dare say it enjoys the sail, but when the sailors get hungry they eat it. If that pig had any sense it would slip down into the boat at the end of the ship and row away."

"My little cousin Molly Gaddum has got a squirrel who has 2 baby squirrels in a hay nest, you cannot think how pretty. They are not much bigger than mice yet ... We have got a tame owl, he eats mice; he sits with a tail hanging out of his mouth."

"My dear Freda, I am staying in such a funny old cottage ... the ceiling of my bedroom is so low I can touch it with my hand, and there is a little lattice window just the right size for mice to peep out of. Then there are cupboards in the walls, that little people could hide in, and steps up and down into the rooms, and doors at every corner; very draughty!"

"Once upon a time there was an old cat called Mrs. Tabitha Twitchit, who was an anxious parent . . ."

The letters are illustrated with little pen and ink drawings, spontaneous pictures which flow on to the page as naturally as words. Rabbits, mice, squirrels, jackdaws, dogs, sometimes Miss Potter herself with umbrella or camera, strolling on the beach, gathering mushrooms, looking at pigs. It is by no means the serious naturalist at work, but the imagination which could picture the sandy recesses of a rabbit hole as furnished with little chairs and tables, and maintain that dried lavender was really rabbit tobacco. (These fantasies, so childish and yet possessing an element of poetic truth, so that they seem always to add to one's knowledge of animal character rather than distorting it, were sometimes indulged in for the amusement of grown-ups as well as for children. Thus, her most sympathetic aunt, Lady Roscoe, was presented with a series of four exquisite little water-colours, displaying the successive stages of a rabbits' winter party; and her "discreet uncle", Sir Henry Roscoe, was startled by the gift of an illustration of a statement in one of his chemical text-books – "N.H.3: The peculiar pungent smell of this compound is noticed if we heat a bit of cheese in a test tube.")

These letters were received with ecstasy by the various children to whom they were written, as we can judge from the fact that so many of the letters have been perfectly preserved – much read and handled, but neither lost nor destroyed – which says much for their appreciation at a time when nobody beyond her family and friends had heard of Beatrix Potter. They were so very popular, in fact, that the thought struck her that she might even make a little book out of one of the letters written to Noël Moore; and she wrote and asked his mother whether by any chance he had kept a letter written eight years before, about Peter Rabbit. Noël *had* kept the letter, and at once agreed to lend it to Miss Potter, so that she might copy it.

She copied the drawings almost exactly, added some others, made the story a little longer, and on Canon Rawnsley's advice submitted *The Tale of Peter Rabbit* to Frederick Warne & Co., prolific publishers of children's books. Alas, Peter Rabbit soon came back to Bolton Gardens, courteously rejected. Disappointed but not discouraged, she tried another publisher, and then another, but with no better success; he was "returned with or without thanks by at least six firms." It became clear that her only hope of seeing *Peter Rabbit* in print was to publish him herself, and accordingly, fortified by Canon Rawnsley, she drew her savings out of the Post Office and got in touch with a printer whose name she had obtained from Miss Woodward – "a friend at the Natural History Museum with whom I was working; her father, Dr. Woodward, edited the *Geological Magazine*, and she knew something about engraving and printing." The engraving and printing cost her eleven pounds.

The form of the book was decided according to her ideas of what a small child's book should be – very small itself, little more than five inches by four, with only one or two simple sentences on each page, and a picture every time one turned over. It was, in fact, very much like Noël's letter, except that there was more of it, and the frontispiece (old Mrs. Rabbit administering camomile tea) had been lightly washed with colour. By December 1901 the little book was ready, a modest edition of two hundred and fifty copies, and she was enjoying the pleasure of selling it in fours and fives to her friends and relations at one-and-twopence a copy. "It caused a good deal of amusement amongst my relations and friends. I made about £12 or £14 by selling copies to obliging aunts." The aunts *were* obliging, and she bore this cautiously in mind: still, now that *Peter Rabbit* was actually published, and looking so much more presentable under the flattery of binding and print, it was perhaps worth while just showing him to Warnes again. They had, according to their letter, been "pleased with the designs", and they were the only firm that had softened a refusal with expressions of polite interest. The book by now was selling so well that she was even thinking of a second small edition, and in February 1902 a further two hundred were printed, with a slightly modified text. This second printing was an interim measure, since on 16th December, the day her first edition was published, Warnes wrote and offered to print *Peter Rabbit* if she would do coloured illustrations instead of black and white.

v

Immediately, for the first and perhaps the only time, Bolton Gardens became interesting. There were discussions about royalties, percentages, copyrights, in which Mr. Potter took a portentous part. Even Mrs. Potter betrayed a fleeting interest, sitting through the empty mornings at her *secrétaire*, mentioning the little book and its success in letters to friends. And upstairs on the third floor, in the room which still had nursery bars in the window, Beatrix Potter was sitting at the table with bent head, writing to her publishers. "It is going off very well amongst my friends and relations, five at a time ... had you decided *not* to go on with it, I would certainly have done so myself, it has given me so much amusement. I showed it this morning to some ladies who have a bookshop in Kensington, who wanted to put it in the window, on the spot; but I did not venture to do so – though I would have been much interested."

There were so many things to be thought of and decided that there was hardly time to turn round. Mr. Potter was laying down the law, and she had a helpless feeling that she was very ignorant, unversed in the ways of publishers. Would it be advisable to consult Canon Rawnsley before she ventured further? And the drawings – surely they would be better drawn afresh, now that they were to be coloured? "I am perfectly willing to redraw the whole if desired ... I did not colour the whole book for two reasons – the great expense of good colour printing, and also the rather uninteresting colour of a good many of the subjects, which are most of them rabbit brown and green." Three-pence apiece, to be sure, was "very liberal" as regards royalty, but then who would the copyright belong to? "I must apologise for not understanding, but I would like to be clear about it ... I am aware that these little books don't last long, even if they are a success; but I should like to know what I am agreeing to ... I have not spoken to Mr. Potter, but I think, Sir, it would be well to explain the agreement clearly, because he is a little formal, having been a barrister."

The letters went backwards and forwards between Bolton Gardens and Bedford Street, discussing blocks, processes, colours, the advisability of improving the original drawings. "I know a little about copper, as my brother etches

Eastwood Dunkeld
Sep 4th 93

My dear Noel,
          I don't know what to
write to you, so I shall tell you a story
          about four little rabbits
                    whose names were—

Flopsy, Mopsy   Cottontail

and Peter

They lived with their mother in a
sand bank under the root of a
big fir tree.

'Now, my dears', said old Mrs Bunny
'you may go into the field or down
the lane, but don't go into Mr McGregor's
garden.'

Flopsy, Mopsy & Cottontail, who were good
little rabbits went down the lane to gather
blackberries. but Peter, who was very naughty

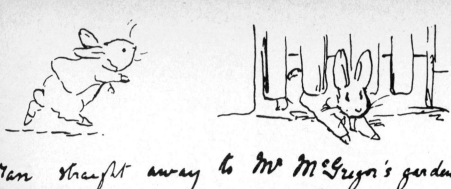

ran straight away to Mr McGregor's garden and squeezed underneath the gate.

First he ate some lettuce, and some broad beans, then some radishes, and then, feeling rather sick, he went to look for some parsley; but round the end of a cucumber frame whom should he meet but Mr McGregor!

Mr McGregor was planting out young cabbages
but he jumped up & ran after Peter waving
a rake & calling out 'stop thief'!

Peter was most dreadfully frightened &
rushed all over the garden, for he had
forgotten the way back to the gate.
He lost one of his shoes among the cabbages

and the other shoe amongst the potatoes.
After losing them he ran on four legs &
went faster, so that I think he would

have got away altogether; if he had not
unfortunately run into a goose berry net
and got caught fast by the large buttons
on his jacket. It was a blue jacket with
brass buttons, quite new.

Mr McGregor came up with a basket which
he intended to pop on the top of Peter,
but Peter wriggled out just in time,
            leaving his jacket behind,

and this time he found the gate,
slipped underneath and ran home
safely.

Mr McGregor hung up the little jacket & shoes for a scarecrow, to frighten the black birds.

Peter was ill during the evening, in consequence of over eating himself. His mother put him to bed and gave him a dose of camomile tea,

but Flopsy, Mopsy, and Cottontail
had bread and milk and blackberries
for supper.   I am coming
back to London next Thursday, so
I hope I shall see you soon, and
the new baby   I remain, dear Noel,
yours affectionately,
                              Beatrix Potter

on it, and have had some experience of printing." (Was she remembering the old printing press in the loft, or some maturer experiment?) "I do not know if it is worth mentioning, but Dr. Conan Doyle had a copy for his children, and he has a good opinion of the story and words." The book was to sell at a shilling (or at one-and-six if gilt-edged), and she was warned not to expect extravagant profits from so humble a price. She was not in the least discouraged. "I should like to take the opportunity of saying that I shall not be surprised or disappointed to hear that the figures work out badly for the first edition of *Peter Rabbit*." Warnes were dissatisfied with one or two of the drawings, particularly those of Mr. McGregor. Perfectly sure of herself where animals were concerned, she was conscious of great weakness in drawing the human figure, and was eager to improve them. "I am very sorry that I cannot call as I am going to Scotland to-morrow morning; my brother has made his arrangements, and I don't want to miss travelling with him. It is most provoking that I could not see the drawings before going, as I think I could very likely do them better there, as there is a garden. Would you be so kind as to post me the two that are the worst? I should be very glad to try them again; any that you are not satisfied with ... The book seems to go on of itself; I had requests for nine copies yesterday from three people I do not know."

Arrived in Roxburghshire, where her brother Bertram (as sick of Bolton Gardens as she was herself, and beginning to have his doubts about the future of art) had decided to take over a small farm as the most extreme change he could think of, she asked his opinion on the drawings, and stalked the farm servants, whom she was too shy to ask outright to be her models. "My brother is sarcastic about the figures; what you and he take for Mr. McGregor's nose was intended for his ear, not his nose at all ... The people are very suitable here, if one was not afraid of them, especially the cook." (Mrs. McGregor, in the private edition, had been a woeful failure.) "If I cannot manage any other way, I will photograph her in the right position, and copy the photograph. I never learnt to draw figures ... The rabbits", she added, reassuringly, "will be no difficulty." But soon even the rabbits were giving trouble, and her letters sped with anxious frequency from Scotland. "I wish that the drawings had been better ... I am sorry to have made such a muddle of them. 'Peter' died, at nine years old, just before I began the drawings, and now when they are finished I have got another young rabbit, and the drawings look wrong."

But the worries were not really serious, and it was all absorbing. In the homely atmosphere of her brother's farm, where Bertram in his quiet way seemed to be tasting his first experience of freedom, her imagination welled up suddenly in all its purity and freshness, and every detail of her surroundings, the potting-shed, the cucumber frame, the geraniums on the window-sill, became invested with a sort of innocent and cheerful poetry, stimulating both to vision and memory; so that before *Peter Rabbit* was properly off her hands she was already sketching out ideas to illustrate a little story she had heard about a tailor, when she was staying with one of her remoter cousins near Gloucester.

CHAPTER
FOUR

The House in Bedford Square

i

The visit to Gloucester had been almost an adventure, for Beatrix had gone there with her cousin, Caroline Hutton, and had had to show some independence to do so. Miss Hutton, who had been staying in London, had suggested to Mrs. Potter that Beatrix might return home with her to Harescombe Grange, near Stroud, and this suggestion had met with disapproval. Beatrix was nearly twenty-eight at the time, and might have been supposed old enough to please herself; and indeed, Mrs. Potter did not actually forbid; but she gave permission very grudgingly, assuring Miss Hutton that Beatrix would never stand the journey, and would certainly faint in the train. "I had not been away independently for five years. It was an event. It was so much an event in the eyes of my relations that they made it appear an undertaking to me, and I began to think I would rather not go. I had a sick headache most inopportunely, though whether cause or effect I could not say, but it would have decided the fate of my invitation but for Caroline, who carried me off." Her cousin Caroline,

THE HOUSE IN BEDFORD SQUARE

who later became Mrs. Clark of Ulva, in old age still clearly remembered the argument and struggle. "I am always glad," she wrote in her eighties, "that in spite of her mother's objections I managed to get her to my old home. She said B. was so apt to be sick and to faint; and I, regardless of the truth, said I was quite accustomed to all that; and of course she could do most things, quite long walks included."

Caroline was some three years younger than her cousin, and held all sorts of radical and free-thinking views which Beatrix found stimulating, if rather outrageous. They talked at night in their dressing-gowns, brushing their hair, and Beatrix decided that Caroline was "a pickle". She "talked of labourers, their miserable wages of eleven shillings a week, their unsanitary cottages, their appalling families and improvidence." She disliked the clergy and spoke boldly against religion. She even thought somewhat slightingly of marriage, which was preposterous. Such feminist views, wrote Beatrix in private, were "the only flaw that I can find in Caroline. Latter day fate ordains that many women shall be unmarried and self-contained, nor should I personally dream to complain, but I hold an old-fashioned notion that a happy marriage is the crown of a woman's life, and that it is unwise on the part of a nice-looking young lady to proclaim a pronounced dislike of babies and all child cousins." Disconcerting, too, was Caroline's father, who was inquisitive and a busybody – "a not very active magistrate, it is more a matter of meddling in small things". She was a little afraid of him, he asked such unnerving questions. "I could not help speculating how many lies I had told him, for he required sudden answers to unexpected questions, and moreover they had to be shouted ... One question which nearly overset me was whether my mother brushed her own hair. This was levied at her servants, Lancashire servants, the history and duties of our domestics, and had we a maid? Now I fortunately did not say so, but my mother's hair takes off."

In spite of small alarms, however, no mishap occurred on this pleasant visit, though Beatrix was a little feverish over her father's second-best camera tripod, which she had been allowed to borrow, and which she was terrified to use in case she scratched it. With its aid she photographed the coachman's children with their rabbits, and went sightseeing with great zest all over the neighbourhood – into old churches, to a cider and perry mill (where she was shocked to see snails being shovelled into the press with the pears), and with special delight into all the old cottages and farms where her cousin had acquaintance.

One afternoon, when some ladies came to tea, she heard a curious story concerning a small tailor in Gloucester who was said to have left a coat cut out, but not made up, in his shop one Saturday; and who, the following Monday, had found it finished all but one buttonhole, and had been startled to see, pinned to the fabric, a scrap of paper on which some unknown person had written, "No more twist." Beatrix listened but said nothing, following her usual habit; but a few days later, when the family drove into Gloucester in the carriage, she asked casually which was the street in which the tailor was supposed to live, and to everyone's amusement sat down on a doorstep and began to sketch it.

The next day she asked her cousin to take her into some more old cottages in and around Stroud, and so made a number of sketches of interiors; of an old settle by the fire, a four-poster bed with faded hangings, a dresser full of crockery, and several fireplaces. The tailor himself she did not find until later, when walking one day through some mean streets in Chelsea she saw through a window exactly what she wanted – an old man in spectacles sitting crosslegged on a low counter, stitching at a garment and surrounded with pieces of stuff. She walked past, pulled a button off her coat, returned and went into the shop. While the tailor worked at this small repair she was able to have a long look at him, and at the snippets and odds and ends that surrounded him; the tape-measure, the tailor's "goose", the brass bowl of water; and carried away more details for her story. The story itself was then written, and the pictures painted, for Noël Moore's sister, Freda, who was in bed with some childish ailment; and *The Tailor of Gloucester*, contained in a stout exercise book with pasted-in illustrations, was sent to Wandsworth with a dedicatory letter –

> My dear Freda,
>   Because you are fond of fairy tales, and have been ill, I have made you a story all for yourself – a new one that nobody has read before.
>   And the queerest thing about it is – that I heard it in Gloucestershire, and that it is true – at least about the tailor, the waistcoat, and the
> "No more twist!"

With *Peter Rabbit* already successfully in hand at Warnes', it was natural that she should wonder whether *The Tailor of Gloucester* too would not make a book. She decided that it would, and that it would be a better thing altogether than *Peter Rabbit*. Still, she did not show it to Warnes, having an idea that they would not be interested in a second book so soon; or that they would want to alter it, or cut out the nursery rhymes, or otherwise disapprove of what she now thought of as her "mouse book", and to which she had become attached; so she went back to the original printers and engravers of *Peter Rabbit*, and herself paid £40 for a coloured private edition of five hundred copies.

The first edition of *The Tailor of Gloucester* is an interesting curiosity to those who became familiar with Warnes' version in the nursery. It is longer; the pictures are not all the same; and it contains a great many more jingles and nursery rhymes, sung by the rats and mice of Gloucester on Christmas Eve. It remained Beatrix Potter's own favourite among all her books, but at the time of printing she was afraid she had made a failure. "I will send you the little mouse book as soon as it is printed," she wrote to Norman Warne. "Except the children's rough copy, I have not showed it to anyone, as I was rather afraid people might laugh at the words. I thought it a very pretty story when I heard it in the country, but it has proved rather beyond my capacity for working out. All the same it is quite possible you may like it . . . things look less silly in type."

A week before Christmas 1902 she was able to send him a copy from Bolton Gardens. "I send the little book. I hope that at all events you will not think the story very silly . . . I undertook the book with very cheerful courage, but I have not the least judgment whether it is satisfactory now that it is done. I'm afraid it is going to fall rather flat here." Norman Warne's immediate appreciation, tempered with criticism, must have reached her by return of post, for two days later she was writing again: "Thank you for your letter about the mouse book. You have paid it the compliment of taking the plot very seriously; and I perceive that your criticisms are just, because I was quite sure in advance that you would cut out the tailor and all my favourite rhymes! Which was one of the reasons why I printed it myself . . . If it is a success," she added, rather wistfully, "it might be improved and reprinted some day. At present it is most in request amongst old ladies . . ."

ii

It was agreed to wait and see how it went off in the private edition, and in the meantime there were discussions, eager and yet diffident on her part, about a second published book. She still could not believe that her own ideas and fantasies about animals could appeal to children in general, and took it for granted that the very best she could hope to do was to follow Randolph Caldecott. "We go to the Lakes for three months, tomorrow," she wrote to Norman Warne; "I will try to bring one of the frames of Caldecotts to Bedford Street in the autumn; I have been looking at them a good deal . . . It may sound odd to talk about mine and Caldecott's at the same time, but I think I could at least try to do better than *Peter Rabbit*, and if you did not care to risk another book, I could pay for it. I have sometimes thought of trying some of the other nursery rhymes about animals, which he did not do . . . I very much enjoyed doing the rabbit book. I would go on with it in any event because I want something to do . . . I did not mean to ask you to say you would take another book."

She had already done a few water-colour drawings to illustrate nursery rhymes and had sent them to "a small drawing society"; she now wondered whether Norman Warne would consider them good enough for a book, since some of the drawings had pleased the society's members. "I notice that those with a bit of landscape are the favourites. Nobody cares for the cocks and hens; and it comes rather near Caldecott's Cat & Fiddle, and comparisons are undesirable . . . I will go on with it on approval if you are undecided, or for myself if you decline it." She had shown him, too, an illustrated letter that she had written nearly ten years before to Noël Moore's brother, Eric, and which had always been a favourite in the Moore family. "I should like to do Mr. Jeremy Fisher too, some day, and I think I could make something of him; though I am afraid your remark that the story is very *interesting* must have been sarcastic!" But soon she had decided that the next best attempt would be a "squirrel book"; she had been visiting more cousins, the Hyde-Parkers, at Melford Hall in Suffolk, and had been interested in the tame squirrels roaming about the place; and remembering the legend about the American squirrels who went down the river on little rafts, using their tails for sails, she brought them together in imagination with that disagreeable owl of her brother's, who used to sit with a mouse's tail hanging out of his mouth.

Very soon *The Tale of Squirrel Nutkin* was taking shape, and she was trying it out, in rough copybook form, on various children. "The words of the squirrel book will need cutting down, to judge by the children here; I have got several good hints about the words. I only hope the gamekeeper will succeed in getting a squirrel before I leave on Monday; I did not find my friends' squirrels at all right when I tried to draw them." Old Brown, the sinister owl of the island to whom the squirrels paid tribute, had somehow become Old *Mr.* Brown by the time the pages were in proof, and she was writing eagerly and at length to Norman Warne about this detail. "Do you really wish to put in all those 'Mr's'? Perhaps they strike me as being out of place because we had an aversion to the original (who was *not* an owl) and we always called him 'Old Brown.' The squirrels should address him as 'Old Mr. Brown' to show extra politeness."

Squirrel Nutkin appeared in the summer of 1903, and was an immediate success. The author had the pleasure of receiving her first letters from child readers, forwarded from Bedford Street. "I have had such comical letters," she wrote to Norman Warne, "from the children about 'scell nuckin' – it seems an impossible word to spell. But they say they have 'red' it right through, and that it is 'lovely' – which is satisfactory. I shall always have a strong preference for cheap books myself, even if they did not pay; all my little friends happen to be shilling people. I do dislike the modern fashion of giving children heaps of expensive things which they don't look at twice."

iii

The pleasures of work and the satisfactions of success were raising her spirits, and giving her a certain measure of independence. She not only, now, had a little money of her own, specially precious for being her own earnings; she had also an occupation, an objective; publishers to visit, business to discuss, a little world of activity which was hers alone and not dependent on her parents. She began to hope that this happy state of affairs might be allowed to continue. "I had been a little hoping," she wrote tentatively to Norman Warne, when *Squirrel Nutkin* was out, "that something might be said about another book, but I did not know that I was the right person to make the suggestion! I could send you a list to consider; there are plenty in a vague state of existence, and one written out in a small copybook which I will get back from the children and send to you to read. I had better try to sketch this summer, as the stock of ideas for backgrounds is rather used up. I would very much like to do another next winter."

But at this, it seems, Mr. and Mrs. Potter made some objection; she was spending too much time over her little books, or going too often to Bedford Street, or straining her eyes, or getting too independent ... Whatever it was, the publishers' invitation to call at Bedford Street to discuss *The Tailor of Gloucester* and any other stories she had in mind, had to be refused, though evidently with a sense of humiliation. "I have to apologise for not having answered your letter, and I regret that I cannot call at the office again before leaving town. If I had not supposed that the matter would be dealt with through the post, I should not have mentioned the subject of another book at present. I have had such painful unpleasantness at home this winter about the work that I should like a rest from scolding while I am away. I should be obliged if you will kindly say no more about a new book at present." There had evidently been a row, and it was not the first time that Warnes had been made aware that she had difficulties at home; indeed, it would have been hard to remain unaware of it, since even Beatrix, most respectful and filial of daughters, had been fairly frank on this point in a postscript to Norman Warne more than a year before, in the midst of the negotiations for *Peter Rabbit*. "If my father happens to insist on going with me to see the agreement, would you please not mind him very much, if he is very fidgetty about things. I am afraid it is not a very respectful way of talking, and I don't wish to refer to it again; but I think it is better to mention beforehand he is sometimes a little difficult. I can, of course, do what I like about the book, being thirty-six. I suppose it is a habit of old gentlemen; but sometimes rather trying."

Though proud of her achievements, as they might have been of a clever child who could recite and play the piano, the Potters seem to have been made uneasy by the tiny measure of independence which success had given her. The fact that she would soon be forty made no difference to their sense of their own authority, and they mistrusted the influence of Bedford Street, and were suspicious of her brightened spirits and new friendships. Their suspicions were not without foundation. Miss Potter had made friends with all the Warnes and their various children and families, and her friendship with Norman, the youngest and only unmarried son of old Mr. Frederick Warne, was of a steadily growing sympathy and warmth which seemed almost to hint at marriage. The Potters saw the danger, and were alarmed. They would not have said, explicitly, that they did not wish her to marry; but they thought it impossible not to regard publishing as a trade, and on those grounds objected to her marrying a publisher. This attitude is so incomprehensible today, and is so purely a product of their class and time, that it needs some elucidation. Even so, it remains obscure, for the Victorian rich middle class, though it hoped for moneyed and imposing marriages for its daughters, did little that was practical to bring those marriages about, and had none of the upper class's frankness about the matter. Girls of the Potters' class were not "brought out"; they had no share in the life of society which, if they had been born higher up in the scale, would have been manipulated to show them off to best advantage and provide them with husbands. Nor were they, on the other hand, allowed any of the freedoms which were among the compensations of humbler life. They were not allowed to find their own husbands through casual encounters, and their world had nothing corresponding to society's machinery for bringing young people together. In Beatrix's case, which was extreme, the subject of marriage was for the most part prudishly avoided, though always with the tacit assumption that if ever she *did* marry it would be solidly, and at a level out of reach of the infection of trade, on which subject the Potters were very wary and sensitive.

iv

The Warnes were unlike the Potters in every way, and Number Eight Bedford Square, the big house where some of them lived and all of them congregated, had nothing whatever in common with Bolton Gardens. The house had belonged to Mr. Frederick Warne, the founder of the firm, and his widow still lived there, surrounded by her sons and daughters and their young children. Not all of them inhabited the house: Harold Warne, who had succeeded his father as head of the firm, and Fruing, the second son, were married and lived elsewhere, and Edith, too, was married, leaving only Norman and Millie to share the roomy and graceful and endearing house with their mother; but the whole family, even to its smallest members, was always converging on Bedford Square for visits, holidays, birthdays, Christmasses and festivals, so that the general impression is of a happy, crowded, free and easy household, in which children and young people and high spirits chiefly predominated. To Beatrix this family life was a revelation. She had been invited to Bedford Square fairly early in her relationship with her publishers, and, her acute shyness once overcome, had been delighted to find that the three brothers of Bedford Street, the "Dear Sirs" of her many anxious and diffident short letters, had for a mother a merry-tempered old lady in a white cap trimmed with mauve ribbons, and a gentle-mannered unmarried sister, Millie, who was almost as shy and retiring as Beatrix herself, and as unobtrusively ready to offer friendship. In this household, where the children of his brothers and sister were constant visitors, Norman Warne, the youngest, was the favourite uncle. He it was who uncomplainingly assumed the red robes and hood and flowing white beard at Christmas parties, speaking through the whiskers in a muffled voice and pretending to be immensely put out when one of his nieces recognized him in spite of all, and ran up and kissed him in the midst of it because it was "only Uncle Norman." His was the magic lantern which beguiled them on winter evenings after tea, and his the dark untidy workshop in the basement where fretwork and carpentry were engaged in, and dolls' houses and cages for mice constructed. He was quiet and very gentle in manner, and seemed destined to remain a bachelor, having reached his middle thirties without falling in love; and this in spite of the fact that his mother, who loved her children to marry and provide her with grandchildren, was anxious that he should choose a wife and settle down, and was always pointing out "nice girls" to him for the purpose. But he was shy with women and clung to his bachelor pursuits, preferring at week-ends to go boating on the Thames with his brother Fruing, or to go hunting moths with him in the Pangbourne woods, with his butterfly net and satchel.

With Miss Potter, however, he was friendly and at ease, perhaps because she was shy herself, and blushed easily, and was such a little oddity when she came to visit him in Bedford Street with her rosy cheeks and bright blue eyes, her sensible boots and umbrella. He, of the three brothers, was the one who most immediately recognized her quality, perceiving the artist under the well-to-do amateur, and she responded to his appreciation with gratitude. Very soon her letters ceased to be addressed impersonally to the publishers and are written to Norman, the only exceptions being those which, owing to their business matter and his position as head of the firm, are more conventionally addressed to Harold; and through the letters to Norman, brief and businesslike and formal though they are, a new note is increasingly discernible. It is as though she had become aware that she had found a being not unlike herself, with whom she could freely and spontaneously discuss her work and her experience of life, in all confidence that the smallest detail would be sympathetically received, and thought worthy of comment.

"I ought to make something good of the coat," she wrote early in 1903, being now engaged on a fresh version of *The Tailor of Gloucester* for Warnes, and busy with new illustrations; "I have been delighted to find I may draw some most beautiful 18th Century clothes at the South Kensington Museum. I had been looking at them for a long time in an inconvenient dark corner of the

Goldsmith's Court, but had no idea they could be taken out of the case. The clerk says I could have any article put on a table in one of the offices, which will be most convenient." So the pictures of the embroidered coat and waistcoat, which in the original water-colours are so fine that they cannot be fully admired without a magnifying glass, and which are among the greatest charms of the Warne version of *The Tailor of Gloucester*, were drawn from show-case specimens in the "V. and A." which are probably still there.

Soon she was writing with amusement to Norman Warne to tell him that the little book had been seriously reviewed in an unexpected quarter. "Did you ever happen to see a review of the *Tailor* in *The Tailor & Cutter*, the paper which the mouse on the bobbin is reading? I have just been calling on my funny old tailor in Chelsea, and he said he had showed his copy to a traveller from *The Tailor & Cutter*, and told him about my drawing his shop, and they had 'put in a beautiful review'!" *Peter Rabbit*, Warnes had discovered to their annoyance, had appeared in a pirated edition in America, and she hoped "they have not got hold of a copy of the mouse book also; but perhaps the private edition is not worth stealing."

The little books as they were written were discussed step by step with Norman Warne, who had a gentle, tactful way of offering criticism, and who was always ready to help with practical advice. In this way he became closely associated with the writing of several of the books, especially *The Tale of Two Bad Mice*, for which he was partly responsible. During Beatrix's visit to Gloucestershire, two mice had been caught in a cage-trap in the kitchen of Harescombe Grange, and she had rescued them from the cook and brought them home and tamed them.

She named them Tom Thumb and Hunca Munca. Tom Thumb seems never to have developed much personality, since he is never mentioned again in her letters once he has been brought home, and one suspects that he probably soon escaped from her home-made cage, and passed to a harder and more adventurous life in the Bolton Gardens basement; but Hunca Munca, the female mouse, showed great character from the first, and revealed an affectionate disposition and a truly housewifely nature, so that she became a pet as well as an artist's model. "I wish 'Johnny Crow' would make my mouse a little house," Beatrix wrote to Norman Warne; "do you think he would if I made a paper plan? I want one with glass at the side before I draw Hunca Munca again. Mine are apt to be rickety." A cage was constructed with a glass front, a ladder, and an upstairs nest, and the mice were installed; and suddenly presented themselves to Miss Potter's imagination as the perfect characters to people another of Norman Warne's ingenious constructions – the dolls' house he was making for his little niece, Winifred Warne, and which Beatrix examined and admired in the finishing stages when she visited his basement workshop.

The Tale of Two Bad Mice was planned out between them in the highest spirits; a flaxen-haired doll and "a doll dressed like a policeman" were borrowed from the Warne children, and Norman Warne undertook to find a Dutch doll for the cook, and doll's-house food, and other useful properties. "Thank you so much for the queer little dollies," Miss Potter wrote from Bolton Gardens, "they are just exactly what I wanted, and a curiosity, coming from Seven Dials ... I will provide a print dress and a smile for Jane; her little stumpy feet are so funny. I think I shall make a dear little book of it, I shall be glad to get done with rabbits . . . I shall be very glad of the little stove and the ham; the work is always a very great pleasure anyhow." In a few days' time a box of doll's-house food had arrived from Hamleys'. "I received the parcel from Hamleys' this morning; the things will all do beautifully; the ham's appearance is enough to cause indigestion. I am getting almost more treasures than I can squeeze into one small book." But the charm of doll's-house food and furniture was irresistible. "The little dishes are so pretty I am wondering if I have made enough of them? Shall I squeeze in another dish? I regret the roast duck being left out! . . . I have bought a gilt bookcase for 8½d.; I wonder what is the colour of the Enc. Britannica, the advertisements don't say; it might be one of the things that would not go into the mousehole." (And indeed, it is, as you will see if you look in the picture.)

The doll's house itself by this time was installed in the nursery of Fruing Warne's house at Surbiton, and the suggestion was made that she should do her drawings there; but at this point Mrs. Potter scented danger, and there was a brief struggle. "I should like to show you the mouse book," Beatrix wrote to Norman Warne; "I have planned it out, and begun some drawings of Hunca Munca – I think you will like them. I was very much perplexed about the doll's house. I would have gone gladly to draw it, and I should be so *very* sorry if Mrs. Warne or you thought me uncivil. I did not think I could manage to go to Surbiton without staying to lunch; I hardly ever go out, and my mother is so exacting I had not enough spirit to say anything about it. I have felt vexed with myself since, but I did not know what to do. It does wear a person out." To his reply, that everyone would be only too delighted if she and Mrs. Potter would come to lunch, she responded in the dispirited tone of one who knew Mrs. Potter better than he did. "I don't think that my mother would be very likely to want to go to Surbiton. You did not understand what I meant by 'exacting'. People who only see her casually do not know how disagreeable she can be when she takes dislikes. I should have been glad enough to go."

Go, however, she could not, and had to content herself with drawing the doll's house from photographs. "I will manage to make a nice book somehow. Hunca Munca is very ready to play the game; I stopped her in the act of carrying a doll as large as herself up to the nest. She cannot resist anything with lace or ribbon; she despises the dishes. I have had so very much pleasure with that box, I am never tired of watching them run up and down. As far as the book is concerned, I think I can do it from the photograph and my box; but it is very hard to have seemed uncivil." Nothing if not thorough, Norman Warne had photographed the Surbiton doll's house inside as well as out. "The inside view," Beatrix wrote, "is amusing – the kind of house where one cannot sit down without upsetting something, I know the sort! I prefer a more severe style."

The book was finished in the course of 1904, and dedicated to Winifred Warne, "the little girl who had the doll's house"; it appeared soon after *The Tale of Benjamin Bunny*, which had been done as a sequel to *Peter Rabbit*, and had kept her so long concerned with the same animals that she was "glad to get done with rabbits." "I think I have done every imaginable rabbit background," she wrote to Norman Warne from Fawe Park, Keswick, where she was now moored for three months with her parents. ("Our summer 'holiday' is always a weary business.") "I had a funny instance of rabbit ferocity last night. I had been playing with the ferret, and then with the rabbit, without washing my hands. She (the rabbit) is generally a most affectionate little animal, but she simply flew at me, biting my wrist all over before I could fasten the hutch. Our friendship is at present restored with scented soap. Little Lucie in Newlands," she added, "is delighted with Nutkin." (Lucie Carr, with whom Beatrix Potter had made friends in her solitary walks, was one of the small daughters of the Vicar of Newlands. A new book, and one of her best, was to come of this friendship.) In *Benjamin Bunny*, though the rabbits were her own, she had been obliged to borrow a cat, and now she shared with Norman Warne her amusement over the cat's owner. "I was asked to pass a message to the publisher about the tail of the cat. Its owner wants you to be assured that its real tail is even larger ... It belongs to old Sir J. Vaughan, late police magistrate, and he is so very feeble I am afraid he will never see the book. He is very funny about the Tailor; he says I ought to have punished Simpkin."

By this time a new book was under way, inspired by an encounter between Lucie of Newlands and Miss Potter's tame, affectionate, much travelled hedgehog, Mrs. Tiggy-Winkle. *Squirrel Nutkin* had done well, and she felt that a story about a hedgehog – especially such a comfortable, clean, good-tempered and fastidious hedgehog – would be equally attractive to children. ("I am rather surprised to hear about *Nutkin*," she had written to Norman Warne after receiving a royalty statement; "it seems a great deal of money for such little books. I cannot help thinking it is a great deal owing to your spreading them about so well ... It is pleasant to feel I could earn my own living.") The hedgehog was proposed to Norman Warne. "I think 'Mrs. Tiggy' would be all right. It is a *girls'* book; so is the

Hunca Munca; but there must be a large audience of little girls. I think they would like the different clothes." Six weeks later, when she had returned from the family holiday in the Lakes with the story worked out and a portfolio of sketches of Cumberland backgrounds under her arm, there was a lull. "I have not begun on the hedgehog book yet, I am ashamed to say; but I think it is not a bad thing to take a holiday. I have been working very industriously drawing fossils at the museum, upon the theory that a change of work is the best sort of rest! But I shall be quite keen to get to work on the books again."

Within a few days she was making her first drawings of Mrs. Tiggy-Winkle, who did not care overmuch, apparently, for posing. "Mrs. Tiggy as a model is comical. So long as she can go to sleep on my knee she is delighted, but if she is propped up on end for half an hour, she first begins to yawn pathetically, and then she *does* bite! Nevertheless she is a dear person; just like a very fat, rather stupid little dog." There was no question of dressing up such a difficult model in the print dress, mob cap and apron which she wears in the story, so a dummy had to be constructed to serve instead. "The hedgehog drawings are turning out very comical. I have dressed up a cotton-wool dummy figure for convenience of drawing the clothes. It is such a little figure of fun; it terrifies my rabbit; but Hunca Munca is always at pulling out the stuffing. I think it should make a good book," she added, "when I have learnt to draw the child." (She was well aware of her weakness in drawing human figures and faces, and indeed Lucie, though she took infinite pains with her and used several models, is the book's only failure.)

No detail of the story's progress was too slight to discuss with Norman Warne, and always in the letters there is the same atmosphere of sympathy and amusement quietly shared. "I do not think that rhyme is right grammar," she wrote, *à propos* of the little song which Mrs. Tiggy-Winkle sang at her ironing, "it is the 'no' that throws it out. If it were

> 'Smooth and hot – red rusty spot
> Never here be seen – oh!'

that would be all right. She is supposed to be exorcising spots and iron stains, same as Lady Macbeth; the verb is imperative."

The little animals themselves were always a matter of interest and concern. Poor Hunca Munca, who had been so obliging a model for *The Tale of Two Bad Mice* and had taken a destructive interest in Mrs. Tiggy-Winkle, met a violent death soon after the hedgehog book was finished, afflicting Beatrix Potter with the grief of a real bereavement and some bitter self-reproach, since it was her own playing with the little creature, and her amusement at Hunca Munca's acrobatics, which had caused her death. "I cannot forgive myself for letting her tumble. I do so miss her. She fell off the chandelier. She managed to stagger up the staircase into your little house, but she died in my hand about ten minutes after. I think if I had broken my own neck it would have saved a deal of trouble."

Mrs. Tiggy-Winkle, who was already old as hedgehogs go when her book was begun, survived another year: her end was related in letters to Millie Warne. "I am sorry to say I am upset about poor Tiggy. She hasn't seemed well the last fortnight, and has begun to be sick, and she is so thin. I am going to try some physic, but I am afraid that the long course of unnatural diet and indoor life is beginning to tell on her. It is a wonder she has lasted so long. One gets very fond of a little animal. I hope she will either get well or go quickly." And a fortnight later, "I might have come up this afternoon, but I have got a sad job trying to finish a drawing of poor little Tiggy. She has got so dirty and miserable I think it is better not to have her any longer; and I am going away for a few days so it is best to chloroform her first. She is not fit to be on anybody else's hearthrug, and it is very nasty here. She has always been such a scrupulously clean little animal." Mrs. Tiggy-Winkle was buried in the back garden of Bolton Gardens, with regret and tears.

v

"I wish another book could be planned out before the summer," Beatrix Potter wrote to Norman Warne at the beginning of June 1905, "if we are going on with them. I always feel very much lost when they are finished." And a few days later, "I do so *hate* finishing books, I would like to go on with them for years." It is clear that the books themselves, and the delight of the work, were not the only things she had come to prize, and that she dreaded losing. The friendship with Norman Warne, the sharing of ideas, the long easy sympathetic correspondence, had become the pivot on which her inner life now turned, and only her intense reserve concealed from everyone, even from her watchful parents, the depth of feeling which the relationship had stirred. In the summer of 1905, however, even the Potters had to know. Norman Warne proposed, and Miss Potter accepted him.

They were both approaching forty. Their friendship had grown steadily through four quiet but eventful years, and in temperament they seem to have been ideally suited. But the idea of union with a publisher affronted the Potters, and they set the whole weight of their authority against it. The next few months were an emotional and deeply painful period. Beatrix Potter was the most respectful and dutiful of daughters: she did not question her parents' right to dictate to her in this matter, and it even cost her some sacrifice of principle, as well as a great deal of guilty misery, to oppose them in it. But she thought their objections to Norman Warne unreasonable, and felt that her life's happiness was at stake. "Publishing books," she said to one of her Gloucestershire cousins, "is as clean a trade as spinning cotton"; but this heresy was uttered in confidence, scarcely above a whisper; almost nobody outside Bolton Gardens and Bedford Square knew what was going on, and the lacerating struggle went on in secret.

What this defiance of her parents cost her, we can never know. But it was an achievement, and marked her first real independence, almost her spiritual growing up. Regretting the necessity to go against their wishes, treating them throughout with complete deference, she showed a firmness which even a Crompton need not have been ashamed of. Though her parents would not agree to it and there could be no public announcement, she quietly proclaimed herself engaged, and openly wore a ring.

During the difficult weeks that followed she was constantly at Bedford Square, where she was received with affectionate sympathy by old Mrs. Warne, and made much of by the children. Fruing Warne's little girls were told that they must now call Miss Potter "Auntie Bee", and that she and Uncle Norman were going to be married.

The children accepted her joyously, though she was not, to them, without her intimidating aspect. Winifred Warne, "the little girl who had the doll's house", and who became Mrs. James Boultbee, wife of a parish priest in Tolleshunt Major in Essex, remembers her at this time as "someone to be reckoned with, someone who would demand a great deal of one in the way of character, and be unsatisfied with less than the best. We had kind aunts, and charming aunts, and silly aunts, but she was someone to look up to and live up to." Winifred's mother, Fruing's wife, was inclined to laugh a little over "Miss Potter's utter lack of vanity – her plainly done hair, and sensible boots and umbrella"; and Winifred's nurse was scornful of Miss Potter's inexperience when she one day helped to dress the little girls in the nursery – ("My nurse's remarks showed what she thought of literary people. *Peter Rabbit* did not weigh in the balance against drawers put on back to front"); but her acceptance at Bedford Square was kindly and complete, and it was there, during the troubled summer of 1905, that she had her first experience of what happy human family life could be.

The experience was brief. Norman Warne, who had never been robust, fell suddenly ill. He would not at first consult a doctor, and when finally he did so it was discovered that he was in an advanced stage of leukaemia and beyond help. He died at the end of August.

The blow to Beatrix Potter was not less heavy from its having to be borne, for the most part, in silence. Few of her friends had been told of her engagement to Norman Warne; it could not be mentioned at home. Only to Millie Warne, with whom she had achieved that rare and difficult thing, a steady and loving friendship, and to whom she now signed herself in letters "your affectionate sister", was she able to indicate, from the depths of her reserve, what it had meant to her. "I am sending you," she wrote to Millie a few days after Norman's funeral, "a copy of the sketch I did the last evening in the barley field at Llanbedr." (She had been here, in Merioneth, when Norman's written proposal of marriage had reached her.) "I try to think of the golden sheaves, and harvest; he did not live long, but he fulfilled a useful happy life. I must try to make a fresh beginning next year." And a few weeks later, when she had gone to spend some days with her aunt, Lady Roscoe, at Bath, where Sir Henry was taking the waters, she wrote again: "I find the names of the streets rather melancholy here. Do you remember Miss Austen's *Persuasion*, with all the scenes and streets in Bath? It was always my favourite, and I read the end part of it again last July. On the 26th, the day after I got Norman's letter, I thought my story had come right, with patience and waiting, like Anne Eliott's did . . ."

Her story was not to "come right" for another eight years. In the meantime there was work, which had given her life its one complete satisfaction; and far away in the north, in that hilly fragment of Lancashire which lies between Westmorland and the sea, there was the modest refuge which (with what hopes and aspirations one can only guess) she had been creating for herself for some time past. For the next few years she buried herself in both.

CHAPTER
FIVE

Hill Top Farm

i

In the summer of 1905, during the long family holiday at the Lakes, Beatrix Potter had taken the unexpected step of buying a farm. Her earnings, together with a little legacy from an aunt, had accumulated into a comfortable sum which it seemed prudent to invest; and this common-sense aspect of the affair, as of a sound speculation, made it possible for her to complete without much remark a purchase which, to her, had a far deeper significance. It was a new experience for her to have money of her own. "I wish I was not always short of money," she had written in 1892, before she had earned anything, and three years later had recorded with some excitement her first acquisition (if it could be so described) of actual capital. "My father gave me rather an extraordinary present, viz., certain bonds of the North Pacific Railway which have paid no interest since April '93, the company being in the hands of the receivers." The gift had been exciting, if nothing else. "The broker advised me to hold on as I was young, but considering I have had the rheumatics, and there was no particular prospect of any interest, I thought I would get out of it . . . I did not of course lose on the transaction, because it was a present." So she had sold the shares. "It is something to have a little money to spend on books, and to look forward to being independent, though forlorn." Now, to her incredulous delight, she had money of her own, which she could invest as she chose.

Summer by summer she had come to know the country between Windermere and Coniston by heart; the Potters had rented houses in and around the village of Sawrey several times, and Beatrix had made friends with the village children, and given them her books. It was then, as now, a green, placid and fertile part of the Lake District, "very pretty hilly country, but not wild like Keswick or Ullswater", good farm land rising in gentle folds above Lake Windermere: and it was here, among pleasant stone-walled hay-fields and steep little pastures, that she heard of the impending sale of Hill Top Farm. She acted quickly. She had known the village of Sawrey since 1896, when her parents had rented a house called Lakefield (now Ees-Wyke), and she had written in her journal, "I was very sorry to come away, in spite of the broken weather. It is as nearly perfect a little place as I ever lived in, and such nice old-fashioned people in the village ... Perhaps my most sentimental leave-taking was with Don, the great farm collie. He came up and muddied me as I was packing up Peter Rabbit at the edge of dark. I accompanied him to the stable-gate, where he turned, holding it open with his side, and gravely shook hands. Afterwards, putting his paws solemnly on my shoulders, he licked my face and then went away into the farm."

At one end of Sawrey village is a small inn, the Tower Bank Arms (which you may see in *The Tale of Jemima Puddle-Duck*), and immediately behind it, reached by a wicket gate in the high wall and a long sloping garden path (which appear several times in *The Tale of Tom Kitten* and on page 33 of *Pigling Bland*), there was the small, ordinary, roughcast and slate-roofed farmhouse, facing away from the village and over its own rick-yard and farm buildings to gently rising pasture crowned with woods. In every respect unpretentious, the place had a quality of its own. Its simple outline was filled in with many of the homely details of farmhouse life which had charmed her as a child: herbs and flowers bloomed together beside the path; there was an untidy pink rose straggling across the face of the house and a beehive set in a sheltered niche in the wall; the kitchen had a good flagged floor, and there was a clean dairy; and the small mixed farm – a few cows and sheep and pigs and a scattering of poultry – was so very modest that she felt that in undertaking it she was running no risk.

The buying of Hill Top Farm was more, however, far more to Beatrix Potter than a speculation. It was a symbol, representing more than one smothered element in her nature. It stood for important decisions and delicate choice, and though decisions and choice produced their fruit only after many years, her emotions about Hill Top were to the end so complex and intense that the sensation of that first break-away, that grasping of life in the country that her heart chose, perhaps never completely faded. She was choosing, like Bertram, to be a farmer, in however partial and incomplete a way; and this in itself implied a rejection, quiet but emphatic, of the life she had had to live for forty years. There can be little doubt that Bertram encouraged her in this. Out of sight on his Border farm and as quiet as a mouse, he had made a busy and useful life for himself, of which only Beatrix knew the true complexion. There was no question of her being able to break away as completely as Bertram had done; such mature freedom was beyond the reach of unmarried daughters, and not to be reconciled with her strong sense of filial duty; but a little farming property bought as an investment, almost a hobby, and visited occasionally, was nothing outrageous, and passed practically unnoticed during the months that saw the struggle over her engagement.

The choice of the Lake Country, too, had its origin in the heart. She had loved it from those first glimpses in childhood, and it lay for her still under that golden haze of the imagination which enchants for ever the first miraculous countryside which the town child discovers. "My brother and I were born in London ... but our descent, our interest and our joy were in the north country." And in the north country, as Bertram in the Border Lowlands, so Beatrix in that strip of high Lancashire in Westmorland chose to be.

Once she had deliberately set her foot there, and the little farm called Hill Top was her own, she fell more wholly in love with the Lake Country, and her feeling for it became passionate and possessive. The forthright simplicity of the people, the homeliness of the life, the satisfaction to be drawn from farming pursuits and the enduring beauty of the hills, evoked such a response from the very bedrock of her nature that it was like the striking of a chord; and out of this harmony, achieved with difficulty and when her life was already more than half spent, came the brief expression of her small but authentic genius – book after little book for the very young, possessed of the shapeliness, the poetry and the texture of perfect lyrics.

When Beatrix Potter first bought Hill Top Farm there was no question of her making it her permanent home;

or, if there were, she kept it to herself. The plan was that she should put in a farm servant or "hind", and manage the property from a distance, visiting it when she could; and this in effect she did for the next eight years. The tenant farmer in possession was one John Cannon, a pleasant man very little older than herself, with a wife and two children. He had not been long in Sawrey himself, and was finding it difficult to make both ends meet when the farm was sold over his head to Miss Potter, who gave him notice. A closer acquaintance with the Cannons, however, changed her mind. In spite of her sheltered life she had a certain native shrewdness and was a judge of character. At all events she knew an honest man when she saw one, and instead of giving him notice, invited John Cannon to value all his own stock and implements, which she bought at his price, enjoying the painstaking fairness with which he weighed every truss of straw and considered every penny; and left him in possession as her farm manager or foreman – to be, as it is locally called, her "hind". This was the beginning of a happy relationship which lasted without interruption for the next twelve years. The Cannons were a part of Hill Top when she first saw it: they remained to initiate her into farming life and to form the comfortable background of her new-found privacy.

By the next summer, almost fully recovered from the illness which had followed the griefs and stresses of that wretched winter, she was busy with alterations to the farmhouse, spending at Sawrey every moment that could be snatched from the family holiday at Keswick. She built on a small wing for the farmer's quarters and a new dairy, reserving the farmhouse proper for herself and adding a large room where several of her brother's paintings were set as panels in the walls, and which was known as the library. "I had rather a row with the plumber," she wrote to Millie Warne, whom she kept minutely informed of all developments, "– or perhaps I ought to say I lost my temper! The men have been very good so far; if he won't take orders from a lady I may pack him off and get one from Kendal ... I *don't* want to come back with the household at the end of September. If I come back then to London, either I will begin a cold, or the cook will give notice, or *something* will prevent me going back to Sawrey, and I want so much to have a good month there, to garden and get extra fat before winter."

ii

Her activities at Sawrey were, sure enough, soon interrupted by further family visiting, this time to Gwaynynog, near Denbigh, to stay with her Uncle Frederick Burton, possessor of another cotton fortune and a large house and beautiful estate. Under the charm of her new enterprise her spirits were recovering, and over the surface of her letters to Millie Warne the old quiet unstressed humour begins to pass again like a faint ripple. "It is warmer here," she wrote from Gwaynynog; "what it will be like in the course of the evening I tremble to think, for there is an immense fire in the gun-room, which my uncle inhabits. It is a little panelled room, very snug in winter; and I shall proceed to draw one of the guns after supper ... Considering he is over eighty and has been run over this summer I think he is wonderful ..."

Among the formal garden and solid comforts of Gwaynynog her thoughts were on the little farm garden at Sawrey: "I am going to get some of the wild daffodil bulbs which grow in thousands here. They grow about Windermere, but there are none in my orchard, though plenty of wild snowdrops"; and she was back at Sawrey as soon as she could escape. "It is beautifully fine here at last – regular autumn weather with heavy dew at night and gossamer all over the grass in the morning ... I am feeling a bit knocked about: I brought back a cold from Wales ... The waitress had a violent cold at Gwaynynog: a nice girl, but always goes about with her mouth wide open, so there was no escape ... I wonder whether I shall do any sketching, or waste all my time gardening! It is rather too early to transplant, but I mean to stick in sticks with labels where things are to go."

This time, accompanied by her friend Miss Woodward, she was able to stay in lodgings in the village while the local builder probed the structure of Hill Top. " I have had an amusing afternoon thoroughly exploring the house. It really is delightful – if the rats could be stopped out! There is one wall four feet thick, with a staircase inside it: I never saw such a place for hide and seek, and funny cupboards and closets. The beds seem all right, she has had a fire once a week. Tabitha Twitchit" – the farmhouse cat – "is so extremely pleased to see me; I am afraid she is pleased *not* to see the hedgehog, which she disliked." "The first thing I did when I arrived was to go through the back kitchen ceiling ... The joiner and plasterer were much alarmed, and hauled me out. I was very much amused. It was a very bad ceiling ... Cannon," she finished up triumphantly, "has bought sixteen ewes, so there will be lambs next spring!"

"I am just in time to overlook the other chimney stack

with great interest. He burrowed into the back of it this morning without any downfall, thank goodness. It is also four foot thick, and full of chaff and hay pulled in by the rats . . ." Mrs. Cannon had been driven nearly distracted by the rats before Miss Potter came, and now they promised to become a problem. "The rats have come back in great force; two big ones were trapped in the shed here, besides turning out a nest of eight baby rats in the cucumber frame opposite the door. They are getting at the corn at the farm: Mrs. Cannon calmly announced that she should get four or five cats – imagine my feelings! – but I dare say they will live in the outbuildings." By the following week the rats had perceptibly advanced, with Miss Potter and the Cannons contesting every inch of ground. "The cats have not arrived yet, but Mrs. Cannon has seen a rat sitting up eating its dinner under the kitchen table in the middle of the afternoon. We are putting zinc on the bottoms of the doors – that and a cement skirting will puzzle them." They were, it seems, sufficiently puzzled, though not altogether defeated, for in a house so old and thick-walled, full of little passages under the floors and in the very structure, it was almost impossible to trace their hiding-places, and the rats had been a long time in possession. They remained for some months longer an enemy which, though diminished, had always to be reckoned with. "I had out the mattresses on the garden wall at the farm . . . Mrs. Cannon was to sew them up again in a day or two, for fear of the rats. We must try to keep them out next autumn; they got in before I had had the holes cemented. It is indeed a funny old house, it would amuse children very much." And even two years later, when the rats at Hill Top had been turned superbly to account and *The Roly-Poly Pudding* had been published, she was still able to send

authentic news of Samuel Whiskers to little Winifred Warne, for whom his story had first been roughly sketched out in a copy-book.

Dear Winifred,

I said last Christmas I was afraid I should see a great deal more of Mr. Samuel Whiskers; but I am glad to tell you he is still living at Farmer Potatoes'. He only comes now and then up to Hill Top Farm. He never came near the place for months, because we had a wonderful clever black cat, called Smutty. She was such a good rat-catcher! But alas, poor Smutty went for a walk one night and she did not come home again . . .

No sooner had Smutty disappeared than there began to be swarms of mice! And one evening there was a visit from Mr. Whiskers. I was sitting very quiet before the fire in the library reading a book, and I heard someone pitter-patter along the passage, and then someone scratched at the outside of the library door. I thought it was the puppy or the kitten, so I took no notice. But next morning we discovered that

Mr. Whiskers had been in the house. We could not find him anywhere, so we think he had got in – and out again – by squeezing under a door. He had stolen the very oddest thing! There is a sort of large cupboard or closet where I do my photographing; it is papered inside with rather a pretty green and gold paper; and Samuel had torn off strips of paper all round the closet as high as he could reach ... I could see the marks of his little teeth. Every scrap was taken away. I wonder what in the world he wanted it for? I think Anna Maria must have been there with him, to help, and I think she must have wanted to paper her best sitting-room! I only wonder she did not take the paste brush, which was on a shelf in the closet. Perhaps she intended coming back for the brush next night. If she did, she was disappointed, for I asked John Joiner to make a heavy hard plank of wood to fit into the opening under the door, and it seems to keep out Mr. and Mrs. Whiskers.

From then on it seems the rats were kept out of the house, and confined their depredations to the farm, where they still, like Mr Samuel Whiskers, indulged their delicate appetites with great cleverness. "A most painful tragedy happened last night," Beatrix Potter wrote to Millie Warne. "I woke up – for a wonder – at the noise of a poor chicken screaming. It stopped, and it was extremely cold; in short, I did *not* get out of bed. I went directly I got up and found a horrid big old rat in the hutch on the lawn. It was eating one chicken and had hurt two others . . . The dogs killed the rat, and the lame ones are recovering. But next time I hear chickens at night, I shall turn out. I feel ashamed of myself; I was half asleep." And during the cold spring several years later, when Samuel Whiskers had long been one of the most successful of her animal villains, she was still reporting, this time to Harold Warne, the abominable successes of "that accomplished thief". "The chickens are deplorable in the hail and rain – and last ill-luck is that a rat has taken ten fine turkey eggs last night. The silly hen was sitting calmly on nothing, Mr. S. Whiskers having tunnelled underneath the coop, and removed the eggs down the hole."

iii

Hill Top could be enjoyed for only a week or two at a time, when a visit could be somehow squeezed into the family programme, and her parents could spare her. During the long summer holiday, which was now always spent in the Lake District in one large furnished house or another, she stayed with her parents and made her way over to Sawrey on every possible occasion. "The lake and woods," she wrote from Windermere, "look lovely in the evening, when I get down to the ferry. I go over to Sawrey about four days a week; it is an easier distance than from Helm last summer, but it is a pretty long walk back. I go there on the Coniston coach in the morning and come back after tea." She was absorbed in her garden, in the half-grown lambs which would soon be going to the autumn fairs, in the litter of pigs which were Cannon's hope and pride. She was alive to all the affairs of the village, and not averse from taking a truculent part in them. "There are several rows going on," she wrote to Millie Warne, while Hill Top was being got ready for occupation, "but I am not in any of them at present, though much inclined. I think I shall attack the County Council about manure. I am entitled to all the road sweepings along my piece, and their old man is using it to fill up holes."

She had made garden-gate acquaintance with most of Sawrey, and in this first autumn of possession, when the cottage garden of Hill Top, soon to bloom in such apparently effortless profusion, was being planted in the half-random, half-instinctive manner for which she had a gift, she rarely came home through the village without begging a clump of pinks, a tuft of thrift, a cutting of lavender. "I have received more plants; it is a time of year when there are clearances and bonfires – I am receiving half the 'rubbish' in the village gardens . . . I wonder," she added, "how many places they still thresh with a flail? On wet days like yesterday one hears it all day long, thump, thump, like the corn in the Bible."

By the following summer the house was all but finished. "I don't know how I shall tear myself away in a fortnight. Another room has been got straight – the front kitchen, or hall, as I call it. I have not meddled with the fireplace, I don't dislike it; and besides, it is wanted for the next book." (She was already minutely sketching the inside of the house for *Tom Kitten* and *The Roly-Poly Pudding*.) "I have got a pretty dresser with plates on it, and some old-fashioned chairs; and a warming pan that belonged to my grandmother; and Mr. Warne's bellows, which look well." Every chair, every tea-cup had its charm because the place was her own, and for the same reason the smallest details of the farm were irresistible. The letters from Sawrey, so different from the many written elsewhere, convince one that here, in her brief intervals of freedom, she was satisfied and happy. "There is a show at Hawkshead on Tuesday; Mrs. Cannon is going to show butter ... and a loaf of bread. Also the collie" – Kep, of whom Jemima Puddle-Duck was "rather in awe" – "but he hasn't a chance, his head is the wrong shape. I have been photographing this morning, photographing the lambs before they depart – Oh, shocking! It does not do to be sentimental on a farm. I am going to have some lambskin hearthrugs."

The problem of tender-heartedness, always a distressing difficulty to the novice, had to be faced, and Beatrix Potter faced it with the practical matter-of-factness which she herself attributed to her north-country blood; so that the killing of animals, that disagreeable essential of farm life, was philosophically accepted, though sometimes with a shudder when she had established friendly relations with them as models. She was interested, in particular, in drawing her pigs, and from time to time added to the sketches which later were to form the basis of *Pigling Bland*. "I have done a little sketching when it does not rain, and I spent a very wet hour *inside* the pig-sty drawing the pig. It tries to nibble my boots, which is interrupting." "I was rather overdone with the head yesterday," she wrote, after drawing and modelling a sucking pig which had been killed for Christmas. "The poor little cherub had such a sweet smile, but in other respects it was disagreeable. It is rather a shame to kill them so young; one has no sentimental feelings about a large bacon pig."

The pigs, great favourites with John Cannon, were becoming increasingly important to the little farm. "The two biggest little pigs have been sold, which takes away from the completeness of the family group ... But their appetites were fearful – five meals a day and not satisfied." "The pigs are mostly sold, at what drapers call a 'sacrifice'. They seem to me to have devoured most of my potatoes before their departure. I was extremely amused during my drive in the trap; Cannon kept pointing out cottages – 'Do you see that house? They've bought one pig! Do you see yon? – they've bought *two* pigs!' The whole district is planted out with my pigs; but we still take an interest in them because if they grow well we shall 'get a name for pigs.' Such is fame!"

Pigs, poultry, sheep and even cattle were slowly increasing while Miss Potter, under John Cannon's unhurried tuition, learned to be a farmer. "The butcher has just persuaded me," she wrote to Millie Warne, "to put in a shilling raffle for a large black Galloway bull, for the benefit of a convalescent home – a singularly inappropriate combination. What an awful thing if one happened to draw the monster!" But it was not long before she had her own Galloways at Hill Top, and was able to write with pride about "an inconsiderate cow who had kept them up till four in the morning. The calf," she added, "was a nice one; it brings the herd up to seventeen head!" Even the prolonged rain of a very cold February could not damp her enthusiasm or undermine her certainty that a farmer's life was what she really wanted, the life she would live to

115

the dregs if she were free to choose. "I find plenty of amusement in any weather. I picked up quite a respectable cartload of firewood this afternoon, and then adjourned to the barn, to chop straw for the cows' supper with a machine . . ."

It was now that Sawrey began to be familiar with the spectacle of Miss Potter, at any season of the year and in all weathers, going about her affairs in the village with sturdy preoccupation, indifferent to appearances. Her feet, like Mrs. Cannon's, would be thrust into the leather-topped, wooden-soled clogs of the district which kept her dry and could be kicked off at the doorstep; her stout tweed skirts would be double or treble, according to the cold; and over her head and shoulders, if it were raining, she was more likely to throw a sack than a coat or shawl. There was something about this little figure, now in her forties growing plumper but still very rosy of cheek and blue of eye, which was singularly attractive; and her forthright unpretentiousness, and the common-sense practical vigour with which she shouldered her growing farm, made Sawrey feel (as she passionately felt herself) that she belonged there – regardless of the fact that she really came from London, and in spite of the north-country preference for distinguishing newcomers for at least a generation as "off-comes", which can be fairly closely translated as "rubbishing foreigners".

As for herself, as Hill Top hardened from a poetic dream into an absorbing reality, her old life – which her sense of duty still obliged her to live for the greater part of the year – was endured with increasing weariness and impatience. In Bolton Gardens, at Gwaynynog, at the various seaside resorts she thought longingly of Sawrey. "I have been rolling the lawn in our back garden today," she wrote from

South Kensington in early spring, ". . . I am very impatient to go up north and plant a few more shrubs before things begin to bud." Later, having reached the Roscoes in Surrey on her round of family visits, "I . . . am going to Windermere with my parents next Wednesday. I have a doubt whether it is the best place for them so early in the year . . . Of course *I* shall like going because I can get over to Sawrey and see the new lambs." And from lodgings in Sidmouth, where they spent a bitter Easter, "I wonder how my poor lambs are getting on, in the snow?"

iv

If Beatrix Potter had been a poet, the eight years following the purchase of Hill Top, when she came and went and experienced her solitary happiness in Sawrey, would have been her lyric years. As it was, being an artist of a different sort, she produced no fewer than thirteen books for children – each of them having in its way the shapeliness and the quality of a poem. These eight years completed her productive period and include all her best work; and of the thirteen books – *The Pie and the Patty Pan, Jeremy Fisher, Tom Kitten, Jemima Puddle-Duck, The Roly-Poly Pudding, The Flopsy Bunnies, Ginger and Pickles, Mrs. Tittlemouse, Timmy Tiptoes, Mr. Tod, Pigling Bland, A Fierce Bad Rabbit and Miss Moppet*, no fewer than six are intimately concerned with Hill Top Farm and Sawrey. It is as though in her own racy, delicate and faintly ironic idiom she had expressed her sense of the deliciousness of her life there – her delight in the old house with its attics and cupboards, in the farmyard, the stone-walled pastures

117

surrounding it, the woods and foxgloves, the lad's love and tiger lilies in the little front gardens of Sawrey, the aroma of bacon and groceries in the village shop. *Jemima Puddle-Duck* is her poem about the farm itself, and anyone who is curious to reconstruct its exact appearance in those days can do so from the pictures in that book. Mrs. Cannon appears at the back door, feeding the poultry; Ralph, her little boy, discovers Jemima's nest under the rhubarb leaves, while Betsy Cannon passes beyond the gate. Miss Potter's cousin, Caroline Hutton, who was now Mrs. Clark and had a little boy of her own, remembered that she "was with her at Hill Top Farm when *Jemima Puddle-Duck* was being written, and went round about with her to find a suitable spot for the nest . . . Kep was a real dog, and his son whom she gave to me was the dearest and cleverest dog I ever had." The idyllic landscape in which Jemima, wearing a shawl and a poke bonnet, is setting out to look for a secret nesting place, is precisely what one sees, even today, after passing through the gate at the bottom of the farmyard. If you turn round, on the very spot where Jemima is standing, you look straight up the farmyard to the house, as in the last picture in the book. In more than seventy years it has hardly changed.

As *Jemima* epitomized the farmyard aspect of Hill Top, so *Tom Kitten* and, still more, *The Roly-Poly Pudding* recorded the garden in the full bloom of spring and early summer, and the loved interior of the house. "I can't invent", she once told Delmar Banner, the Westmorland artist with whom in old age she would sometimes discuss painting, "I only copy'; and whether or not one agrees with her, there is no doubt that Hill Top and Sawrey provided her with exactly the sort of material in which her imagination delighted.

The kitchen range in *The Roly-Poly Pudding* is not there now, since Beatrix Potter replaced it with an open grate, but otherwise the house, even today, is little changed, and she never failed to find amusement in the astonished delight of children who, knowing the book, were shown over the actual rooms and staircase of "Tom Kitten's house". The old dresser, past which Anna Maria ran with her plate of dough, still stands where it did, and the staircase and landing, where Tabitha Twitchit mewed for Tom and Samuel Whiskers trundled the rolling-pin, are still unchanged; only, mounting those stairs with their graceful balustrade and pausing on the landing with its long window and faded claret-coloured curtains, one is surprised by the smallness of the scale. In the book it looks almost imposing: in reality it is a good-sized cottage – a discrepancy which suddenly resolves itself when one realizes that Tabitha Twitchit is, after all, a cat, and that the human scale of curtains and banisters is by comparison stately.

The rooftop view of Sawrey in spring, facing the page on which Tom Kitten "made up his mind to go right to the top, and get out on the slates, and try to catch sparrows", is still not very different from the view one sees today from the staircase window, though Sawrey has grown, and the rooftops are more numerous and the apple-trees fewer; and towards the end of the book, where the author "looked up the lane from the corner, and ... saw Mr. Samuel Whiskers and his wife on the run, with big bundles on a little wheelbarrow, which looked very like mine", there is a faithful view of part of Sawrey, and even a glimpse, in the distance, of Miss Potter herself. (The only other hint at a self-portrait in all her books is in *Pigling Bland*, on page twenty-two – "I pinned the papers, for safety, inside their waistcoat pockets". "I think I shall put *myself* in the next book," she had written in 1910 to a little girl in New Zealand, "it will be about pigs; I shall put in me walking about with my old 'Goosey' sow; she is such a pet.")

The Pie and the Patty-Pan roams about the village of Sawrey, lingering over the tiger-lilies and snapdragons in cottage gardens, glancing into parlours and kitchens, pausing to admire a whitewashed slate-roofed porch covered with purple clematis, and to consider the plants in cottage windows and the pumps in backyards. One or two of the street scenes were drawn in Hawkshead, but the book is Beatrix Potter's praise of Sawrey, and contains many village details that she loved. It is the only book (if we except the dedication of *Benjamin Bunny* "To The Children of Sawrey") in which Sawrey is mentioned by name – " 'A little dog indeed!' " said Tabitha Twitchit disdainfully, " 'Just as if there were no CATS in Sawrey!' " – and Duchess, the black Pomeranian dog who is the heroine of the story, (". . . never much to look at herself," as Miss Potter told her publishers, "though a most valuable little dog") was a Sawrey dog and lived only a stone's throw from Hill Top.

Ginger and Pickles, the last of the Sawrey books, celebrates the actual little village shop, and with such appreciative feeling that its pages almost smell of candles and tea. It is full of sly personal references, designed to please or amuse the people of Sawrey, who had discovered the reason for Miss Potter's absorbed wanderings with pencil and paint-box, and responded with a touching form of local patriotism. "The *Ginger & Pickles* book has been causing amusement," she wrote to Millie Warne. "It has got a good many views which can be recognised in the village, which is what they like: they are all quite jealous of each other's houses and cats getting into a book. I have been entreated to draw a cat aged twenty 'with no teeth'. The owner seemed to think the 'no teeth' was a curiosity and attraction! I should think the poor old thing must be rather worn out." The owner of the village shop was bedridden, and the book was accordingly dedicated "With very kind regards to old Mr. John Taylor, who 'thinks he might pass as a dormouse': (three years in bed and never a grumble!)" "It was all drawn in the village near my farmhouse," Miss Potter wrote to Louisa Ferguson, her little correspondent in New Zealand, "and the village shop is there. Only poor old 'John Dormouse' is dead – just before the book was finished. I was so sorry I could not give him a copy before he died. He was such a funny old man: I thought he might be offended if I made fun of him, so I said I would only draw his shop and not him. And then he said I had drawn his son John in another book, with a saw and wagging his tail" (Mr. John Taylor's son was the village carpenter, and had appeared, disguised as John Joiner the terrier, in *The Roly-Poly Pudding*), "and old John felt jealous of young John. So I said how could I draw him if he would not get up? – and he considered for several days, and then 'sent his respects, and thinks he might pass as a dormouse!' It is considered very like him." (For the likeness one must turn to page sixty-nine – "And when Mr. John Dormouse was complained to, he stayed in bed, and would say nothing but 'very snug'; which is not the way to carry on a retail business.") "Also", Miss Potter added, "it is very much like our 'Timothy Baker', but he is not quite so well liked, so everybody is laughing."

Beatrix Potter was in love with her life in Sawrey, and with the whole of Hill Top. Prudently and steadily she increased her holding there – a few sheep, an extra cow, another field: even, as they came into the market, two other little farms in the village, with fields adjoining; and a white-washed cottage here and there, and a small stone quarry; until, in the course of a few years, she had come to own half the village, and was a person to be reckoned with in Sawrey. But she was not yet free to live the life she loved, and there was no immediate prospect of her being so. "I am on the committee and a determined person," she wrote to Millie Warne in 1911, describing the village row over the coronation celebrations, "but – unfortunately non-resident." She regretted it from every point of view, and must have envied Bertram, with his growing farm and his independence, comfortably out of sight in the Border country; but there were her parents and the domestic life of Bolton Gardens to be considered: and the London of her "unloved birthplace" was still, for three-quarters of the year at least, her home.

v

Meanwhile there were interests, little off-shoots from her now successful and established work, which kept her sufficiently occupied in London. *Peter Rabbit* was being translated into French, by a lady with the splendid name of Mlle. Victorine Ballon; and Beatrix Potter, whose own schoolroom French was of a fairly high standard, was keeping a critical watch on the translation. The very simplicity of the book, and the uncomplicated delicacy of its flavour, made it unexpectedly difficult to translate; it fairly bristled with small and subtle problems. The names of the characters, for instance: was "Pierre Lapin" really the equivalent of "Peter Rabbit"? "I do *not* like 'Pierre Lapin'," Miss Potter wrote, "I should call him 'Pierre Laperau'." And then, more difficult still, "Could the translator suggest French names instead of Flopsy, Mopsy and McGregor?" Mlle. Ballon rose to the challenge with "Flopsaut, Trotsaut, Queue-de-Coton et Pierre", but Mr. McGregor, true to his race, proved inflexible, and even Mlle. Ballon could make nothing more Gallic of him than "Mr. Mac Grégor".

There is something quite irresistible, to an English ear, about these French translations: Mère Lapin is still Old Mrs. Rabbit, as one sees from the pictures, and yet – when "elle traverse le bois et s'en va chez le boulanger, acheter une miche de pain bis et cinq brioches", how mysteriously changed! Her most familiar pronouncements have an astonishing undercurrent – "Un accident affreux arriva à votre pauvre père dans ce maudit jardin. Il fut attrapé et mis en pâté par Madame Mac Grégor." Miss Potter struggled conscientiously with these nuances, writing to Mlle. Ballon, "Please – do not try to keep so near the *English* words: it only spoils the French": and the finished translation is certainly delicious. The sensation of delighted and amused surprise with which sentence after sentence falls on the ear takes one back, perhaps, more nearly than anything else to the emotion of childhood on hearing the Beatrix Potter books read aloud for the first time: and Miss Potter herself, enjoying, like many another author, the complacent experience of reading her own works in French, was made newly aware of their charm. "I like the French translations," she confessed in a letter, "it is like reading someone else's work – refreshing."

While Peter Rabbit was being naturalized in French, German, Spanish, and eventually Welsh, he had already made his appearance in a different medium. Beatrix Potter had once made a Peter Rabbit doll for one of the Warne children, with "some shot in the body and coat-tail. I don't think it will come out," she had written to Norman Warne, "unless the legs give way. Children sometimes expect comfits out of animals, so I give fair warning!" The doll had given so much pleasure that she had thought of manufacturing Peter Rabbit dolls as a side-line, and had taken her idea to a number of London toy factories. Here she came up against an economic reality, which until then had been nothing more to her than a party catchword and an accepted part of the then prevalent Liberal politics. The policy of Free Trade had for years been filling the British market with cheap foreign goods, and the British toy trade had been killed by the import of huge quantities of cheap toys from Germany. The Camberwell doll industry, which had employed skilled female labour for generations, was on its last legs: German dolls had successfully undercut the native product, and wherever Miss Potter went in her search for a live toy factory to undertake Peter Rabbit, she found despondency and unemployment. At the same time, to add insult to injury, pirated "Peter Rabbits" began to arrive from Germany, and were followed by a cheaply made but still recognizable "Squirrel Nutkin". "My father has just bought a squirrel in the Burlington Arcade," she wrote to her publishers: "it was sold as 'Nutkin'. It is prettier than the rabbits, but evidently the same make – I wonder how soon we may expect to see the mice!"

Beatrix Potter began to consider the Free Trade policy of her Radical grandfather with disfavour, and as the question of tariffs had affected the sale of her books in America she became strongly convinced of the necessity for Tariff Reform, and for a brief period, in the months before the 1910 General Election, busied herself with propaganda. The issues of this election were the abolition of the House of Lords veto, the merits of the Budget, and Tariff Reform, with Austen Chamberlain and Bonar Law at the head of the Tariff Reformers: and Beatrix Potter, whose Crompton pugnacity made her very much at home on the Opposition side, and who by temperament and upbringing was an unshakable Conservative, found herself oddly suited by a Tariff Reform campaign in which the Liberal Government was defied by rebellious Tories. (She had always found it easy to accept Mr. Potter's politics. "O, if some lunatic had shot old Gladstone twelve months since!" she had exclaimed fiercely at nineteen, in the privacy of her journal. Supporters of Home Rule for Ireland were "a band of self-interested assassins", while leaders of the unemployed riots of 1885 ought, she had agreed with Papa, "to be hung at once like dogs.") To swell the volume of Tariff Reform propaganda, which – to quote the *Annual Register* of that year – was "conducted not only on the platform and in the Press, but by a host of obscure missionaries" – Beatrix Potter did two things: she wrote and printed at her own expense a characteristically vigorous (though none too clear) argument in favour of Protection, and she drew by hand some scores of coloured posters.

The printed sheet is signed, and was presumably distributed by hand and letter-box throughout the length and breadth of South Kensington to explain the reasons for Miss Potter's opposition to Liberal policy. "A few years ago I invented a rabbit doll which was in demand. I tried in vain to get it made in England. There was not a single British wholesale toymaker left who could undertake the job . . . My doll is now made by scores in Frau H-'s factory in Germany . . . The London toy shops are choked with foreign toys.

"Now the question has reached my books. There has always been very great difficulty about English books in the United States. The States are enormously rich and protected by heavy tariffs. We have no tariff by means of which we might bring the States to reason. They simply laugh at us. My most successful book has been pirated and reprinted by American printers who have never sent me a halfpenny.

"The difficulties about 'copyrighting' an English book in America are now so very great that we are obliged to engrave and print *in* America all copies intended for American use . . . The manufacture and wages belonging to those copies are now lost to England . . .

"It is uphill work, trying to help folk who will not help themselves. Why should I bother myself about the British workman, if he prefers 'Free Trade'?"

Conservative opposition to the Liberal Government's Budget proposal to increase the Land Tax struck an equally responsive chord in her, and having spoken as author and would-be toy-maker she concluded her pamphlet in the character of small landowner. "I have one expensive field which would be liable to the special ½d. on its capital value . . . If the tax is raised I shall be obliged reluctantly to raise the rent . . . I am not a Duke: I bought that field out of my earnings and savings. Also I have no vote!" (It would be amusing to know what she would have done at this point with the vote if she had been offered it, since she was opposed both by temperament and conviction to the idea of Woman Suffrage, and this same year wrote to Millie Warne, "What games there seem to be with the Suffragettes! It is very silly work.") "My grandfather," the pamphlet concluded, "was Radical member for Carlisle, a colleague of Bright and Cobden. In those days the working man had not the Franchise. It is nonsense to pretend that the old bad days of the Corn Laws can ever come back, now that the people have votes. The working man can safely give Tariff Reform a trial without being frightened by the bogey of dear bread."

Beatrix Potter's Tariff Reform posters were small, rough and hand-drawn, and showed a British-made doll in a limp condition – "Poor Camberwell Dolly is dying, Killed by Free Trade." The expense of colour printing had probably decided her to do the posters by hand, and in spite of their simplicity the labour of drawing and lettering several score must have been very great. "I am so busy over the Election," she wrote in January 1910, "my fingers are quite stiff with drawing posters."

Excitement over the election (in which she found herself in political accord with her parents and most of their friends) subsided abruptly into disappointment at the end of the month when the Liberals, headed by Mr. Asquith, were returned once more, though without a working majority. "Organised labour" – to quote once more from the *Annual Register* – "... was, on the whole, for Free Trade ... Unorganized and agricultural labour largely on the other side, to some extent under the influence of the upper class, which was generally strongly against the Budget and in favour of Tariff Reform." Beatrix Potter, still exasperated over her American editions and by what she considered to be Government interference with the small farmer, was confirmed in the Conservative opinions to which she remained attached for the rest of her life: and although she maintained a lasting interest in politics – always from the practical if narrow point of view of the working landowner – she made no further attempt to influence the electorate, so that the year of this memorable election was long distinguished in conversation by the Potter family as "the year when Bee went into politics".

Her books by now were so successful that she had to be increasingly on her guard against infringement of copyright. The American pirated edition of *Peter Rabbit* had meant a substantial loss, both to herself and her publishers; and though her books were now protected by copyright on both sides of the Atlantic, there were lesser piracies from time to time – some deliberate, as in the case of the German Peter Rabbit toys, some unintentional and innocent. "I have had a letter from a Mrs. Garnett, whom I know slightly," Beatrix Potter wrote on one such occasion to her publishers. "She has made a frieze for her nursery out of *Peter Rabbit*, and it is so popular she would like to show it to a paper manufacturer, and she wants to know whether you would object to its being printed? I am so much perplexed by this artless appeal that I have basely advised her to write to *you* ... I should think it would make a very popular nursery paper, but I do not know in the least if Mrs. Garnett can draw? Of course if it were done at all it *ought* to be done by me – but I find it rather awkward to say so ... The idea of rooms covered with badly drawn rabbits is appalling: the American edition would be nothing to it!" On hearing from Warnes on the question of copyright Mrs. Garnett, we may assume, realized that her suggestion had indeed been "artless", and said no more; and a design for a nursery frieze by Beatrix Potter, featuring Peter Rabbit and other animal characters from the books, was submitted by Warnes to a wallpaper manufacturer. "It is very kind of you," she wrote, in reply to their news that they had had a cool reception, "to have taken the trouble to go personally to Sandersons' . . . I am not very keen about selling it to a firm who don't fancy it much . . . I think Sandersons are right in calling the designs old-fashioned; but the books – which are certainly not new art or high art – have sold pretty well!" On second thoughts, however, Sandersons apparently admitted the possibility of success, and eventually made a first printing of the nursery frieze, a revised edition of which has sold steadily ever since. Miss Potter was pleased, and added the small royalty to the revenues of Hill Top.

vi

She yearned for Hill Top and Sawrey more and more. The election had been a passing excitement and had made London interesting, and there were small affairs of copyright and translation which occupied her attention while she was there: but she was now more than ever conscious of impatience, and of a sense of wasted life. While in Sawrey the sheep grazed with their lambs beside them and the haymaking had begun, to sit idle and alone in Bolton Gardens was intolerable. Gradually, advised and supported by Bertram, she had increased her stake in the north: gradually the ties with Bolton Gardens were loosened. The time was coming when she would escape.

In 1909 she had bought Castle Farm, a small property within sight of Hill Top, with a pleasant farmhouse and long low white-washed cottage sitting side by side under the hill, on a narrow grassy lane which ran into the village. The home meadow of Castle Farm sloped down to the road, with a gate at the very point where the Tower Bank Arms confronted the village with Hill Top behind it, so that the fields of the two farms could be conveniently joined while the farmhouses were almost within whistling distance of one another. The purchase was made through a firm of Hawkshead and Ambleside solicitors, W. Heelis & Sons, an old-established family business which had dealt for two generations with the affairs and property transfers of the district; and the partner who dealt personally with Miss Potter and drew up the contract for her was Mr. William Heelis, a quiet, tall, leisurely man of about her own age, in appearance not unlike the poet Wordsworth, who had been born and educated at Appleby and had hardly ever been outside his native Lake Country. Mr. Heelis, who had known all the local farmers and land-owners since he was a boy, was able to give Miss Potter valuable advice in her buying; he could sympathise with her passion for Hill Top and he was helpful over the difficult laying of a water supply to the new property. She, for her part, understood and appreciated his country tastes and his gentleness, his pleasure in fishing and a little rough shooting when the week's work was done, the sweet-tempered and courteous manner in which he shouldered her affairs. They were much together over the laying of the water supply to Castle Farm, going out on the hillside to inspect the work in bitter weather: and when Miss Potter caught cold, and went home to Bolton Gardens in the very nick of time before developing influenza, it was Mr. Heelis's friendly letters which kept her in touch with Sawrey, and helped her to keep at bay the two spectres which gloomily haunted her in Bolton Gardens – loneliness and depression.

Her illness was prolonged, and left her weak. Depression

settled on her and was difficult to shake off, for she felt too feeble to face the struggle which she knew must follow when she confessed that Mr. Heelis had made her an offer of marriage. When old Mrs. Warne had died some years before, she had done her best to comfort the solitary Millie. "I wish you had Norman to help you, but we must try to feel it is all ordered. You will all your life have the comfort of remembering you have been the most devoted good daughter . . ." Millie Warne had that comfort, and Beatrix Potter, we must suppose, very earnestly longed for it now: and dreaded to broach, for a second time, a subject so unwelcome to her parents as her own marriage. Still, it had to be faced, if she were ever to enjoy the happiness she longed for, and she forced herself to face it.

Their reaction was precisely what she had expected, and she fell back for a time on her old resource of dogged patience: though perhaps doubting her ability, at forty-seven and in poor health, to repeat the difficult victory of ten years before. There had, however, in this later controversy been an unexpected note. Bertram, emerging from his Scottish retreat to pay one of his infrequent visits to his parents, had been pressed into the fray; and had astonished them, not only by quietly supporting his sister, but by casually announcing that he himself had long ago got married without consulting them, and had been perfectly happy for years with a shop-keeper's daughter.

The struggle, as it had done before, went underground, and was carried on apprehensively and in secret. The early months of 1913 were outwardly the same as any other period in the Potter family; Beatrix was immured in Bolton Gardens and far from well; she had bought yet another little farming property at Sawrey out of her royalties, and her parents were proposing to go to Windermere for Easter;

but under this unruffled surface, with much difficulty and self-reproach on Beatrix's part, the wretched debate between happiness and filial piety dragged on.

It told on her health, and her heart gave warning signals. "I have been resting on my back for a week," she wrote to Harold Warne in March, "as my heart has been rather disturbed . . . I am assured it will recover with quiet." And six weeks later, having at last escaped from Bolton Gardens to Hill Top, "I seem to get on very slowly. I am decidedly stronger, and look perfectly well; but I was completely stopped by a short hill on trying to walk to the next village this afternoon. I believe persevering slow exercise is the best cure . . . I am quite sure I am best out of London, and as my parents have come to an hotel for a holiday (and spring cleaning) I hope they will be satisfied for me to stay here a little longer." Meanwhile she wrote privately to her cousin, Caroline Clark, asking for her advice. "I advised her to marry him quietly, in spite of them," Mrs. Clark remembered: "they thought a country solicitor much beneath them . . . and she had the (now) old-fashioned ideas of duty from children to parents, and to excuse them wrote, 'I see their objections, as we belong to the Bar and the Bench.' "

By midsummer the argument had reached and passed its crisis, and Beatrix was able to write to Millie Warne and tell her in confidence that she and Mr. Heelis were engaged. "Thank you for your kind letter," she wrote a few days later, in reply to her old friend's good wishes, ". . . I have felt very uncomfortable and guilty when with you for some time – especially when you asked about Sawrey. You would be only human if you felt a little hurt! Norman was a saint, if ever man was good. I do not believe he would object . . . I certainly am not doing it from thoughtless light-heartedness as I am in very poor spirits about the future. We are very much attached and I have every confidence in W.H., but I think it can only mean waiting and shall never be surprised if it were for the time broken off." There were, however, no further attempts to dissuade her, and on the fourteenth of October, in the parish church of St. Mary Abbot's, Kensington, Beatrix Potter became Mrs. William Heelis.

The honeymoon was spent at Sawrey, in a furnished bungalow above Castle Farm, where the cottage – bigger than Hill Top and more convenient – was being got ready for them. Hill Top had given Beatrix Potter all the freedom and most of the happiness she had known, but she felt that it was too small and primitive for her husband, and was unwilling to alter it. The rooms at Hill Top were tiny; the Cannons, at their end of the house, lived at close quarters – one could hear their voices through the communicating door and the ring of pails in the dairy – and the only water supply was a pump in the yard. All this, of course, could have been altered, but she loved it too much to change. So Hill Top was kept as it was, the beds aired and the rooms swept and the windows open, while Beatrix Potter made a second home for herself, only the breadth of a narrow field away.

And immediately the atmosphere of her life changes. Calm, and the certainty of sympathy and happiness succeed the divisions and disappointments and enforced patience of her single life. She was by temperament eminently suited to a useful and unpretentious married life, and she knew it. She settled into her new position with touching pride.

"I am sending you belated cake," she wrote to Millie Wane, a week after her marriage, "which I hadn't courage to do before! . . . I am *very* happy, and in every way satisfied with Willie. It is best now not to look back." A week later, as Mrs. Potter was changing servants, there was a summons to London, but the parting from William and Sawrey was not allowed to last long. "My mother is just expecting a new parlourmaid and counts on my being at hand . . . I feel very dumpy without my husband; it was hard luck to have to leave, after only a fortnight; he is coming up for me on Saturday. Now, if you want to get me a nice useful present that I shall always use and remember you by – get me Mrs. Beeton's Cookery, *please*, and write my name in it! Nothing like asking!" In due course Mrs. Beeton arrived in Sawrey, and contributed her share to conjugal life. "I do seem to have let you in for a large solid gift! I had no idea that Mrs. Beeton had grown so stout. I shall be much amused to experiment with her; I already take exception to her direction to fry bacon in a cold pan. Wm. prefers blue smoke before the bacon is laid on the frying-pan. There are probably more disputes over bacon and plain potatoes than any other eatable. I can do both – and very little else!"

As Christmas approached the Heelises became ambitious, and cured hams. "Agnes Anne at the village shop (the original of *Ginger & Pickles*) . . . has done a very awkward thing," Beatrix wrote to Millie Warne, "– sold Cream of Tartar by mistake for saltpetre, and Mr. Heelis rubbed it on the hams. It discoloured them, but I hope may not have done any harm, as the mistake was found out and the hams washed." "It seems strange," she reflected, "to be away at this time of year; but I hope my parents do not mind *much* – I mean not specially on account of the time, as we have never kept up anything different for Christmas to a usual Sunday." Christmas at

Sawrey was made festive by Mrs. Beeton, if nothing else. "The messes – mingled with really elegant suppers – which William and I cooked after the departure of Mary Jane (her real name) are most remarkable. William took a turn at pastry *à la* Mrs. Beeton, but I am of the opinion she recommends the use – or misuse – of more butter than is justified by results. What we do really well are roasts and vegetables. We cooked and ate a turkey and several other birds." The following April she wrote to Millie Warne, "I feel as if I had been married many years."

In those few months her life had undergone a profound change. She was approaching fifty, and all the best of her creative work was done. As Beatrix Potter she already enjoyed a little measure of fame, and was financially independent; but the change from Miss Potter to Mrs. Heelis went far deeper than the name. It was as if, disliking so much about her earlier life that she could hardly bear to be reminded of it, she deliberately buried Miss Potter of Bolton Gardens, and became another person. Mrs. Heelis of Sawrey, who for the next thirty years was to be known as a dominant, shrewd, good-humoured and salty character of the Lake Country, was absorbed in the life which Beatrix Potter had always wanted, and had achieved only by snatches in her possession of Hill Top, and expressed with love and poetic truth in her art. She now, at fifty, consciously possessed it, and the celebrity which she might have enjoyed as Beatrix Potter was cast aside without a thought. From now on she would be a farmer, and Willie Heelis's wife; and by the outbreak of the 1914 war in the first summer of her marriage she was already totally absorbed in her new existence, nourished by hard work and the affectionate, half-humorous contentment which sustained her life.

During the war she described this life in a letter to Miss E. L. Choyce, who had read a complaint in *The Times*, signed "H. B. Heelis", of the shortage of labour on small farms, and had written to offer her services; and one cannot give a better picture of Beatrix Potter's life and character at this time than by quoting it almost in full.

Hill Top, Sawrey.
March 15, 1916.

Dear Madam,

Your letter reached me this morning. Do you mind telling me, are you a girl or middle-aged? I am fifty this year – very active and cheerful; but I am afraid I and my farm-housekeeper are both going to be overworked. I must explain at once that I don't depend on the farm for a living, so some people might not call it real "war work"; but I have farmed my own land for ten years as a business (before and since marriage) and I have got it into such good order it would be a pity to let it go down . . .

This is between Windermere and Coniston; very pretty hilly country, but not wild like Keswick or Ullswater . . . My husband is a solicitor; as there are all sorts of people in the world I may say he is a very quiet gentleman, and I am a total abstainer! We have been two years married, no family. We live very quietly in a cottage separate from the old farmhouse; I have one young servant here. On the farm I have employed a family for ten years – John Cannon, cowman-foreman-shepherd; Mrs. C., dairy woman, farm-housekeeper; Willie C., ploughman . . . My husband helps with the hay, but he is short-handed too.

I have poultry, orchard, flower garden, vegetables, no glass, help with heavy digging, cooking with the girl's assistance. Mrs. C., I and this girl all help with hay, and I single turnips when I can find time ...

It is best to speak straight out; the difficulty with a stranger woman is the boarding. I can see Mr. Heelis doesn't want a lady living here. I don't think a lady would live comfortably (for either party) in the Cannons' back kitchen. There remains the front part of the farmhouse, which I used before I married, and which we still use for spare bedrooms, library, etc ... It is a lovely old house, in fact the furniture and old oak is so good I can only have a careful occupier ... There are two doors through to the farm quarters, but it is complete in every way (except a fixed bath) ...

I don't go out much, haven't time; and the little town seems nothing but gossip and cards. I'm afraid our own special sin is not attending church regularly, not loving the nearest parson; and I was brought up a Dissenter ... I am very downright, but I get on with everybody.

There is a postscript: "Your letter is very earnest: I wonder if you have a sense of humour?" Nothing is more characteristic of her than her pause on this sudden doubt, unless, perhaps, it is her giving it expression.

CHAPTER
SIX

The Beatrix Potter Books

i

With marriage, and the beginning of a new and absorbing
life in Sawrey, Beatrix Potter's creative period came to an
end. Half a dozen books, it is true, were published after
she had become Mrs. Heelis; but these books were for the
most part patched together from sketches and notes which
had lain for years in her portfolios; and they show a marked
falling off from her best work. Set in the midst of her long
life, then, her charming creative period lasted for little
more than ten years; at the end of that time her inner
vision seemed to undergo a change, or her own life began
to absorb her emotions, so that the magic evaporated. The
writing of her stories had always been inseparable from
their illustration; the flavour of the books is tasted equally
and indistinguishably in pictures and text; and it is a
curious fact that from the moment when her eyes began
to fail and she lost her power of fine drawing, her stories
lost their shape, their emotional concentration, and their
poetry.

In those ten years or more, however, of exquisite

achievement she had produced a series of little works impossible to imitate, and without any rival in the field of children's literature. By the end of her life, two generations of children had already been brought up on them, had their imaginations first stirred, their sense of beauty and humour first awakened by these fantasies of her own childhood transformed into works of art. Her books had come to mean as much to the children of America as to the "little people of Sawrey" whom she always remembered; some had been translated into several languages, and their sales had mounted steadily into millions. It is an achievement unprecedented in children's literature, and difficult to match even in wider spheres. What is the secret of her excellence? Why are the Beatrix Potter books – some of them after sixty years of familiarity – still incomparably the favourites of the nursery, and as well known in their details to at least two generations of adults as traditional fairy tales?

The answer is that most satisfying of all possible answers – that they are good art. A high level of execution, founded partly on a naturalist's loving observation of animal life, partly on an imaginative awareness of its character, lifts her work into a class of its own among children's books. Her water-colours have the beauty and fidelity one might expect in some luxuriously produced set of volumes on natural history, and some of them (the illustrations of *Squirrel Nutkin* are a case in point) might almost be admired without remark in such a context; until some sly detail, faithful to squirrel character but not to squirrel habit, arrests the eye, and we find ourselves in a world where squirrels gather nuts into little sacks, play marbles with oak-apples on a level beech-stump, and cross the breadth of Derwentwater on rafts, using their tails for sails.

This fidelity to animal character is the very strength and sinew of her work. There is nothing grotesque or misleading, however fabulous. All her little hedgerow, farmyard and wainscot animals are conceived with *imaginative* truth, and though they are shrewdly humanized, and their stories told throughout in human terms, there is, imaginatively speaking, not a word of falsehood. We close the books, knowing more about animal and human nature than we did before.

Conveying truth by means of fantasy, enlarging our perception of life by poetic means, is one of the highest functions of art, and it is not extravagant to say that in her small and special sphere Beatrix Potter performed it. She understood and loved the little animals that she drew and painted, and perceiving – perhaps even without being aware, for her response to imaginative stimulus was most innocent and direct – perceiving that invisible thread of sympathy which runs through the whole animal creation, including man, she interpreted her animals in human terms. Displayed in the trappings of their human counterparts, they reveal their own true natures by oblique methods, and we ever after know more about them from having observed their behaviour in significant disguise. Mrs. Tiggy-Winkle, that "scrupulously clean little animal", gets her living by washing and ironing; Jemima Puddle-Duck, laying first in the rick-yard, then under the rhubarb leaves, and finally, in desperation, in the foxy-whiskered gentleman's wood-shed, raises the theme of frustrated maternity almost to the level of a farmyard tragedy, and displays as well – as no other story could better prove – the idiotic innocence of her kind. Mrs. Tittlemouse, the "woodmouse with a long tail", is exquisitely domesticated, a "most terribly tidy particular little mouse, always sweeping and dusting the soft sandy floors" of her burrow, and though mops and brushes are not seriously to be looked for in the holes of woodmice, Mrs. Tittlemouse, inveterate nest-maker, typifies the beautifully observed fastidiousness of her mouse nature.

In the same way Ginger the cat, serving behind the counter and doing grocery accounts, is a figure of pure fantasy, yet his cat nature is thereby delicately underlined. "The shop was also patronized by mice – only the mice were rather afraid of Ginger. Ginger usually requested Pickles to serve them, because he said it made his mouth water. 'I cannot bear,' said he, 'to see them going out at the door carrying their little parcels.' "

Even the clothes in which her animals are so unerringly dressed contribute something, by however improbable a route, to our imaginative understanding of their characters. Mrs. Tiggy-Winkle wears a print gown, a striped petticoat and an apron – of course! one almost exclaims, what else would you expect? – Mr. Jeremy Fisher is dressed, apart from his mackintosh and galoshes, not unlike Mr. Pickwick, and the result is most suitable; and Mr. Tod, as one would predict of that vindictive and sandy-whiskered person, is something of a dandy. It is most interesting, too, to observe those situations in which the animals appear without their clothes: it is never done by accident, but always to stress and as it were recall their true natures – Mrs. Tiggy-Winkle vanishing among the bracken at the end of the story; Jemima Puddle-Duck without her ridiculous bonnet and shawl when she has achieved the dignity of motherhood; most telling of all, the sandy-whiskered gentleman, unclothed, uncivilized, pure fox at last, turning over Jemima's eggs in the wood-shed.

Beatrix Potter's great sense of animal beauty, and the imaginative truthfulness of her approach, saved her from that element of the grotesque which infects nearly all nursery books about animal characters. (It is, of course, easier to caricature an animal than to draw it beautifully, which perhaps accounts for the great preponderance of ugliness and sham naïveté in children's books.) She knew it was quite unnecessary to distort animals and make them "funny" in order to touch the imagination of a child. On the contrary, it was their very beauty, and the seriousness and reality of their little world, which had held her entranced through the long summer holidays of her own childhood, and which was the very basis of their appeal. There was humour enough, of a very delicate, ironical and loving description, in their characters and adventures, without resorting to comicality or any of the vulgar expedients by which children are nowadays amused on a commercial scale. The fundamental difference between the two methods of approach is displayed in the contrast between any of the Beatrix Potter books and the Tiger-Tim-Mickey-Mouse school of children's literature; in the one, a deliberate distortion and comicality is laboured (often most successfully) to evoke laughter; in the other, both the aesthetic sense and the emotions are at once engaged.

One is not consciously aware of these things in childhood: response to the books is simple and direct, and it is not for many years that one realizes how very deeply they have sunk in, what a lasting little pattern they have imprinted at the back of the mind. Beatrix Potter's own emotional response to certain things in childhood has been most subtly and beautifully conveyed – the family lives that go on in burrows and holes, the natural detail of hedge and ditch and kitchen garden, the revelation of beauty and dewy freshness in the northern countryside, the homeliness of its farm kitchens, the cool smell of dairies, the fragrance of baking days – they are all now a part of our own vision. She has made her books, like lyrics, out of emotional experience, and it is this real feeling under the gentle playfulness of the fantasy that strikes so directly home.

The domestic details of north-country farmhouse life are among the things to which Beatrix Potter herself most completely, and, considering Bolton Gardens, most surprisingly responded. A well-scrubbed flag floor, a rag rug of many colours, a saucepan on the hob and a flat-iron heating against the bars of the range, were not objects to evoke any pleasure, one would suppose, in the minds of Mr. or Mrs. Potter; but Beatrix was in love with every circumstance. Nothing, not the pattern of an oven door nor the design of a crochet kettle-holder escaped her, and she dwelt on the household arrangements of Tiggy-Winkle and Tabitha Twitchit as lovingly as a connoisseur on the details of Van Eyck. Anyone, indeed, who has a nostalgia for the special atmosphere and flavour (one might almost say the *smell*, for a well kept north-country farmhouse kitchen *has* a delicious smell which defies analysis) of those Westmorland interiors, cannot enjoy it in imagination more completely than by studying any of Beatrix Potter's books which fall into the "domestic" group; they are perfect records, in their way, of a simple life which still exists on the fells, and which had gone on undisturbed for generations when Beatrix Potter discovered it as a child.

In this world, life centres in the kitchen, round the fire, where Tom Kitten's mother sets her dough to rise under a clean blanket and Tiggy-Winkle airs her linen and heats her irons. There is always a polished steel fender and a rag rug; there are tin canisters along the mantelpiece, a crown-lidded teapot (relic of Edward the Seventh's coronation) on the hob, and a kettle-holder hanging from a nail. Crochet wool antimacassars in faded colours soften the backs of the favourite chair and the hard horsehair sofa under the window. There are geraniums and Creeping Jenny on the sill: and tea, when it is spread on a clean cloth on the kitchen table, will include a nicely baked pie in a pink and white dish, milk in a patterned jug and a pat of yellow butter on a dinner plate. One feels that the dairy, with its stone shelves and whitewash, is not far away, and that upstairs the bedrooms will have flowered wallpapers covering the beams, and will be fresh and tidy, with decent china ewers and basins and cane-bottomed chairs.

Beatrix Potter's female animals, true to the north-country spirit of these loved interiors as well as to their own natures, are all good housewives; they are proud of their comfortable kitchens and best parlours, they do all their own baking and washing and readily turn to spring-cleaning for emotional expression. Even Hunca Munca, in the midst of her wanton destruction in the doll's house, recovers her sense of responsibility in the nick of time. "But Hunca Munca had a frugal mind. After pulling half the feathers out of Lucinda's bolster, she remembered that she herself was in want of a feather bed. With Tom Thumb's assistance she carried the bolster downstairs and across the hearthrug. It was difficult to squeeze the bolster into the mousehole; but they managed it somehow. Then Hunca Munca went back and fetched a chair, a bookcase, a bird-cage, and several small odds and ends . . ." Mrs. Tittlemouse followed Mr. Jackson about with a dish-cloth, "to wipe his large wet footmarks off the parlour floor", and when his messy adventures were over she "got up very early and began a spring-cleaning which lasted a fortnight. She swept, and scrubbed, and dusted; and she rubbed up the furniture with beeswax, and polished her little tin spoons." Flopsy, the mother of the rabbit babies kidnapped by Tommy Brock, does "a complete turn-out and spring-cleaning, to relieve her feelings"; and even Mr. Tod, none too fastidious on his own account, is as careful as Mrs. Tiggy-Winkle would have been to cleanse his house of the badger. " 'I will bring my bedding out, and dry it in the sun,' " said Mr. Tod. " 'I will wash the table-cloth and spread it on the grass in the sun to bleach. And the blanket must be hung up in the wind; and the bed must be thoroughly disinfected, and aired with a warming-pan; and warmed with a hot-water bottle. I will get soft soap, and monkey soap, and all sorts of soap; and soda and scrubbing brushes; and persian powder; and carbolic to remove the smell. I must have a disinfecting. Perhaps I may have to burn sulphur.' " What more could the most scrupulous housewife demand in the way of clearing the air after an objectionable visitor? And Mrs. Tiggy-Winkle, of course, is far more than a washerwoman: she is an accomplished laundress. In her "nice clean kitchen with a flagged floor and wooden beams – just like any other farm kitchen" there is a "nice hot singey smell" and Mrs. Tiggy-Winkle expertly ironing and goffering and shaking out the frills. " 'Oh yes if you please'm, I'm an excellent clear-starcher!' " Only one animal does Beatrix Potter seem to have made, perhaps unjustly, dirty: and that is Tommy Brock: for the badger is a clean animal with fastidious notions in his domestic arrangements, and might well have been admitted to the ranks of the burrow-proud.

ii

There is another element in Beatrix Potter's books which it is diflicult to find elsewhere in children's literature: the deeply felt beauty of the countryside. The lakes, the fells, the stone walls and white-washed farms that she loved are drawn, on their modest scale, almost with the emotional feeling of a Constable: and the freshness and poetry of some of her little pictures (Mrs. Flopsy Bunny, for instance, coming hesitantly across the field and wondering "where everybody was", or the squirrels fishing in the lake at evening and carrying their tribute of minnows through the wood) raises her to a humble but secure place in the British School.

She herself, with the crusty impatience which developed as she grew older, and took pride only in her achievements as a farmer, would not have agreed that her vision had anything at all in common with Constable's, or that it was anything but "rubbish" or "bosh" to link her, however lightly, with the traditions of English art. But it is not unknown for artists to be poor judges of their own work, and one cannot escape the conclusion that Beatrix Potter, who more than once confessed that she could never be sure what was good and what was bad in her own stories, became to some degree also blind to what was best in her painting. As she grew old, she grew steadily more impatient of such discussion. She accepted quite simply the appreciation of children, or of those who had loved her work in childhood and still responded to it emotionally; but any consideration of her painting as "art" was likely to provoke her, in her last years, to a terrifying rudeness. "Great rubbish, absolute bosh!" she wrote to her publishers in the last year of her life, when a sensitive appreciation of her work, written by Janet Adam Smith, had appeared in *The Listener.* The writer of the article had placed her, within the limits of her childish sphere, in "the same company as... Palmer, Calvert, Bewick and a host of earlier English artists," having "in full measure Samuel Palmer's gift of suffusing a landscape with innocence, happiness and serenity," and a capacity for drawing little hedgerow animals "with the affectionate precision that we find in Bewick's wood-cuts." "I revere the names of the immortals," Beatrix Potter wrote to Warnes when, thinking to please her, they had sent her the article, "and I have this much in common with them, that like them I have tried to do my best, and taken satisfaction in so doing, from love of painting ... but to compare the manner of my work with theirs is silliness." To Miss Adam Smith, who also had guilelessly sent her a copy of the article, she wrote that she had read it with "stupefaction", and made it clear, from the asperity of her denials, that she thought she had been accused of copying these artists. Appalled, Miss Adam Smith hastened to reassure her. She had meant only, she explained, that "your illustrations often give the reader the same kind of pleasure as the pictures of these earlier English artists do. I read somewhere the other day that Constable, asked by a friend what he was trying to do to a picture he was working on, said, 'I am trying to put the Dewy Freshness into it'; and that phrase, the Dewy Freshness, did also seem to describe some of your illustrations." But to no purpose: it was clear that Miss Potter now thought she was supposed to have copied Constable. "I have too much common sense," she replied, "to resent a suggestion that my painting manner is not original, but founded on another painter's manner; but I think it is silly to suggest it is founded on Constable – a great artist with a broad style. When I was young it was still permissible to admire the Pre-Raphaelites; their somewhat niggling but absolutely genuine admiration for copying natural details did certainly influence me; also F. Walker and his school, and Hunt"; and concluded with a somewhat tart postscript that "when a person has been nearly thirty years married it is not ingratiating to get an envelope addressed to 'Miss'". No matter; the opinion which an artist or writer holds of his own work is always interesting; but it is unwise to accept it as the only criterion.

The landscapes of Beatrix Potter's books, which are indeed, like Samuel Palmer's, suffused with innocence and happiness, are nearly all in the north country, and many of them can be identified. (*The Tailor of Gloucester* is, of course, an exception; so is *The Flopsy Bunnies*, which was drawn at Gwaynynog, near Denbigh, and *Little Pig Robinson*, which was based on early sketches of Sidmouth, Lyme Regis and Hastings.) Mrs. Tiggy-Winkle lives, as the last sentence in the book makes clear, in "the back of the hill called Cat Bells"; Newlands, Little-Town, Skelghyl are all easily found to the west of Derwentwater. Pigling Bland journeys out of Westmorland into Lancashire and back again; he and Pigwig escape over Colwith Bridge and go to live in Little Langdale; Owl Island, where Squirrel Nutkin lost his tail, is in Derwentwater, and Mr. Tod can "generally be found in an earth amongst the rocks at the top of Bull Banks", which are up above Hill Top Farm.

Timmie Willie travelled in the vegetable hamper to a house in the square at Hawkshead. The beautiful kitchen garden scenes of *Peter Rabbit* are not to be found anywhere together; they are widely scattered. "Peter was so composite and scattered in locality," she wrote to her publishers, when they had sent her a magazine article about her work which was not altogether accurate, "that I have found it troublesome to explain its various sources. If the vegetable garden and wicket gate were anywhere, it was at Lingholm near Keswick; but it would be vain to look for it there, as a firm of landscape gardeners did away with it, and laid it out anew with paved walks ... The lily pond in *Peter* was at Tenby, S. Wales. The fir-tree and some wood backgrounds were near Keswick. Mr. McGregor was no special person; unless in the rheumatic method of planting cabbages. I remember seeing a gardener in Berwickshire extended full length on his stomach weeding a carriage drive with a knife. His name I forget – not McGregor! I think the story was made up in Scotland. Peter Rabbit's potting shed and the actual geraniums were in Hertfordshire" (Camfield Place) "– but what does it matter? I called the garden at Gwaynynog 'Mr. McGregor's garden' when I used it for the backgrounds in *Flopsy Bunnies*; so, as Uncle Fred Burton used to say, 'Leave it at that!' The garden in *Benjamin Bunny* was at Fawe Park, Keswick."

iii

Natural beauty; innocence; "dewy freshness"; these are all elements of Beatrix Potter's work, but they are not the whole. Designed as it is for the very young, there is nevertheless nothing namby-pamby about it. It is completely free from any touch of sentimentality. An unstressed faintly ironical humour is alive on every page, and running below the surface of each narrative is a seam of something which can only be described as *toughness*. Beatrix Potter was deeply aware of the realities of nature; the earth and its seasons, the rhythms of sowing and harvest, of life and death, were her deepest source of emotional life and spiritual strength; and the laws of nature (especially those of pursuit and prey, with which the life of most wild animals is endlessly concerned) are nowhere softened or sentimentalized in any of her stories. Her rabbits tremble with good reason at the thought of Mrs. McGregor and her pie-dish, for that, after all, has been the end of their father. Mr. Tod is a figure of real terror, not only to innocent Jemima Puddle-Duck, who at first is too simple to realize what he is about, but to all the small defenceless creatures of farmyard and wood. "The rabbits could not bear him; they could smell him half a mile off. He was of a wandering habit and he had foxy whiskers; they never knew where he would be next." When Benjamin and Peter, heroic in desperation, creep up to his earth under Bull Banks to try and rescue Benjamin's kidnapped family, the details of that sinister place are not glossed over. "The sun had set; an owl began to hoot in the wood. There were many unpleasant things lying about, that had much better have been buried; rabbit bones and skulls, and chickens' legs and other horrors. It was a shocking place, and very dark." Nor is this all. Peering in at the dark window, which is shut, in search of his little family, Benjamin sees "preparations upon the kitchen table which made him shudder. There was an immense empty pie-dish of blue willow-pattern, and a large carving knife and fork, and a chopper. At the other end of the table was a partly unfolded tablecloth, a plate, a tumbler, a knife and fork, salt-cellar, mustard and a chair – in short, preparations for one person's supper. No person was to be seen, and no young rabbits. The kitchen was empty and silent; the clock had run down. Peter and and Benjamin flattened their noses against the window, and stared into the dusk." Mr. Tod's kitchen is another of those north-country interiors that we have come to know so well, but it is dark, deserted, sinister. It has something in common with Mr. Piperson's kitchen in that other near-gruesome night-piece, *The Tale of Pigling Bland* – the same atmosphere of loneliness and silence, of cruel villainy menacing the innocent. Both stories end with escape in the early morning, and a sense of relief which, after the stifling suspense of the night's adventures, is like sunrise itself after the uneasy dark.

The pursuit and prey theme runs undisguised through many of the tales. Indeed, only from the purely "domestic" stories – *Two Bad Mice, Mrs. Tiggy-Winkle, Mrs. Tittle-mouse, Tom Kitten, The Pie and the Patty-Pan*, is it entirely absent. Johnny Town-Mouse, for all his sophistication, lives in constant danger from the cat, and repeatedly takes shelter, as from an air-raid, in the coal cellar. Tom Kitten runs into hideous danger when he hides up the kitchen chimney on baking day, and gets lost in the flues, which "shows how very unwise it is to go up a chimney in a very old house, where a person does not know his way, and where there are enormous rats." The trout lurks underneath the lily leaf for Mr. Jeremy Fisher; Simpkin hungers after the mice on the tailor's table; and round the corner of any potting-shed or cucumber frame little rabbits are apt to come on Mr. McGregor.

In dwelling on this theme Beatrix Potter was following, more or less consciously, the simple traditional pattern of the fairy tale. Instead of giants and ogres and bad fairies, there are Mr. Tod and Samuel Whiskers to beware of. The results of too great innocence or rashness, in fairy tales or Beatrix Potter's stories, are much the same. The stories point no moral, unless it be that the helpless and the simple, if they are not very careful, may make a meal for somebody else; and *Jemima Puddle-Duck*, as she was fond of pointing out, is really *Little Red-Riding-Hood* re-told. Yet, though Tom Kitten is encased in suet crust and feels the rolling-pin, though the shadow of the pie-dish falls across the rabbits' lives, there are no tragedies. Children, as Beatrix Potter well understood, are willing to be harrowed with suspense, but not with unhappy endings; and our feelings are nowhere wantonly exacerbated. Pigling and Pigwig, who came near to being bacon and hams, escape at last over the county line; Tom Kitten is restored to his family, the dumpling having been peeled off and "made separately into a bag pudding, with currants in it to hide the smuts"; Jemima Puddle-Duck survives to raise her brood.

iv

The quality which most, in the last analysis, distinguishes Beatrix Potter among children's writers (and indeed distinguishes her in a much wider sphere) is her ability to create a special world and fill it with original characters who "come alive". "It does not matter," wrote Lord David Cecil in *Early Victorian Novelists*, "that Dickens' world is not lifelike; it is alive"; and with Beatrix Potter, as with all artists who are genuinely creative, what really matters is the presence or absence of that vital spark. The life in her animal characters is so irrepressible that there are moments, even in reading her letters, when one is willingly convinced that she believed in them herself; that she *saw* the rat ever after as Samuel Whiskers, and the badger as Tommy Brock; and was more than half in earnest when she wrote "Besides – *I* have seen that door into the back of the hill called Cat Bells – and besides *I* am very well acquainted with dear Mrs. Tiggy-Winkle!" She was able, at all events, in letters to children to give later news of her characters than had appeared in the books – a kindness which authors rarely perform for their readers, and which must, in a sense, have been the fruit of her imaginative conviction.

"It is sad to have caused such disappointment!" she wrote in 1915 to a family of unknown children in a Devonshire rectory who had written to complain of the non-appearance of a sequel to *Mr. Tod*. "Though I must say – when I was a little girl, I was satisfied with about six books, three dolls, and a stuffed cotton pig. I think that children now have too many . . .

"I think I saw Tommy Brock's wife last week. I couldn't think who the person reminded me of, and when I read your letter I remembered directly. I am not sure how many of a family there are – lots! and what we call a 'long' family, all ages with some long time between. I believe Tommy Brock is very grumpy with the grown-up ones, and makes them clear off into the woods; and, as you know, he is not often at home himself. Mrs. Badger is rather lighter coloured than he is, rather sandy, with little piggy eyes and a snouty nose, and a not particularly clean house, I should say – *she* finishes wearing out Tommy's celebrated boots. Mr. Tod has been across lately, I smelt him myself; but he had removed before the hounds came."

This imaginative identification of the species with the

particular character is, of course, an easy and natural step in a child's mind. The game which Beatrix Potter so beautifully kept up in her letters was played with great seriousness by hundreds of children who wrote to her at her publishers' address. "I think I have little friends all over the world," she told a correspondent in New Zealand; and to Millie Warne, as early as 1909, she had written, "I hope you will have a pleasant Christmas at Surbiton. I shall devote mine to answering an accumulation of unknown children. I cannot get them done before." Though she could not keep the scores of children's letters which found their way, year by year, to her home in Sawrey, and which came so thick and fast that she confessed herself "plagued with child messages and letters", there were some that she could not persuade herself to destroy; and after her death there was found among her papers a letter from Francis, her cousin Caroline Clark's little boy, the "William Francis of Ulva" to whom, in 1912, *The Tale of Mr. Tod* had been dedicated.

> My dear Cousen B.,
>   Thank you very much for the nice little book. Do you like Timmie Willie – I don't. I and my dog Jack are always killing him. We have great mouse hunts. One day we had a great hunting: one day, I dug and dug till I got a mouse nest – and Jack swooled two mice like pills. We have Samule Whiskers all over the house: he ran over my hanktuhes in the landrey one day, and made them very dirty.

Complete belief in the reality of Samuel Whiskers, and in his presence in the laundry of a Highland house, is no special feat in the imagination of a child. But to give Samuel Whiskers, in the first place, such compelling life, required a deep imaginative conviction in his inventor; and that quality, in common with all other first-rate and sincere artists, Beatrix Potter possessed, and to an eminent degree. "No one," wrote Dickens in the preface to *David Copperfield*, "can ever believe this Narrative in the reading more than I believed it in the writing." It is a condition of success with the novelist, as with any creator of character. It is the clue to the living pulse of Mr. Micawber; it is no less the secret of Tom Kitten.

CHAPTER
SEVEN

The Fairy Caravan

i

Beatrix Potter's brief and exuberant creative period came to an end, as we have seen, with her marriage. It had been a comparatively short flowering, but perfect of its kind, the result of many years of unconscious preparation. Of the four story-books which appeared after her marriage only one, *Johnny Town-Mouse*, which was published in 1918, can be compared in style and spirit with her earlier work. The others, *The Fairy Caravan, Little Pig Robinson* and *Sister Anne*, published ten years later and deliberately addressed to her American public, break away from her own tradition and are in that sense experimental; but they are not happy experiments. Their interest is chiefly that attached to a good artist's failures.

It is easy to see how it happened that Beatrix Potter, when she married, turned away from the original work which had given her celebrity, and produced only these few experiments which would never have seen the light if it had not been for the persuasions of her American admirers. Her heart, now, was in farming, and for the first time, in middle age, she was free to do as she liked and give her life to it. She was already mistress of several small farms; she had sufficient capital to expand, and had become interested in sheep-farming – particularly in the little hardy Herdwick breed – and was learning from the beginning all the technical and practical wisdom that her shepherds could teach her. Her own life, at last, made full and satisfying demands on her emotional capacity; and when we consider that the difficult and hard-working war years were upon her when she had been less than a year married, so that she was obliged to do much of the rough work of the farm herself and even work in the fields, it is not surprising that she had little time or creative energy for fine water-colour painting. "I shall not be able to do much more," she wrote to Fruing Warne, when she had been working on some little pictures for *Peter Rabbit's Almanac*; "these are good, but they try my eyes very much. I can't see to do them on dark days, and the lambing time is beginning, when it is not possible to neglect out of door affairs." "I am written out for story books," she confessed a few years later, "and my eyes are tired for painting." She knew, with a certainty of judgment which did not always serve her, that her best work was done.

Still, there were plenty of unused sketches in her portfolios, and scraps of paper stuffed into the drawers and pigeon-holes of her desk, on which she had scribbled odds and ends of notes about farmyard animals, and scraps of old stories and fragments of nursery rhymes that had once suggested something. There were still some old ideas, too, for illustrating nursery rhymes, (*The Owl and the Pussycat* was one that had always attracted her), and turning traditional fairy-tales into new children's stories. And there were a few ideas for stories, founded on the letters she had written to children more than thirty years ago, which had been discarded, or forgotten.

It is unlikely that she would have made anything out of all these fragments on her own initiative. In 1927, however, an American publisher who was on a visit to England and had discovered her address, paid a flying visit to Sawrey, inspired by the idea that a new *Peter Rabbit* or its equivalent could surely be charmed out of the inventive fancy which had already produced so much. Beatrix Potter received his proposals with surprise. She had not really thought of writing another story, and it would perhaps be disloyal to Warnes if she did so, for a stranger; still, the new publisher's importunity was very flattering, and she had always had a fondness for Americans. They had a way, the most cultured and charming of them, of seeking her out in Sawrey and seriously treating her as a writer of children's literature. They never came, like the less prepossessing Lancashire trippers, by char-à-banc from Windermere, to leave paper bags about or stare at her rudely over the garden gate. "I always tell nice Americans to send other nice Americans along," she had written to a lady from Boston who had asked for permission to visit her. "You come because you understand the books, and love the same old tales that I do – not from any impertinent curiosity." And now there was this demand, by an urgent and very businesslike American, who had left a hundred pounds on the table by way of encouragement. "There has been an alarming visitation," Beatrix Potter wrote to one of her now numerous and always assiduous American correspondents, ". . . an American publisher who took the trouble to come all the way from London in search of a book that does not exist. Alexander McKay. He produces very beautifully illustrated books, there is no question about that. It would vex my old publishers very much, and I don't like breaking with old friends. Possibly I may arrange to have something published in America for the American market only."

The Fairy Caravan, the "something" with which Mr. McKay was eventually rewarded, was not published in England until 1952, apart from a small private printing to secure copyright, and it was Beatrix Potter's wish that it should be confined to America. The reason she gave to her English publishers (who felt rather as Ginger did about the mice when they saw a large new volume of Beatrix Potter stories going into the American bookshops) was that the book would not stand comparison with her better work, and that she did not want it so compared in her own country. To her American friends she explained that the book was too explicit for home consumption – "too personal – too autobiographical – what do you call it?" – its publication in England would spoil her retirement. (In the private edition she appears on the title page as "Beatrix Heelis".)

There seems to have been truth in both excuses, yet both leave something unsaid. She was, in fact, a little sick of her old successes, and was tempted to try her hand at something new. "I believe my attitude of mind towards my own successful publications has been comical; at one time I almost loathed *Peter Rabbit*, I was so sick of him. I still cannot understand his perennial success." A good deal of *The Fairy Caravan* had been lying in her desk for years. She had written the various fragments to please herself; some of it *did* please her; but it was unaccustomed stuff, and she was unsure of its quality. "It is a fact," she wrote to one of her American friends, "that I could not appraise my own manuscript. Sometimes I thought it was a remarkable work; other times I thought it was such absolute bosh I felt shy about having it printed at all." It was quite different from her other books, "stories of a rather different sort which I had no wish to publish in this country ... You may ask, why print them at all, then? I suppose – vanity, and a desire to see them in the dignity of printed type, without the expense of myself paying for the printing."

She had a few copies privately printed in England, to make sure of the copyright, and these she distributed among her friends and neighbours, who eagerly followed up the personal references. "The book is lengthy; but children will be able to have single complete stories read to them. Our shepherd's children turn over the pages looking up the references to animal friends again and again. It is very comical how seriously the village has taken it."

The identity, then, of the book's characters was clearly enough known in and around Sawrey, and she had no objection to her American readers comparing *The Fairy Caravan* with her best work. We must look further to explain the defensive, half-secret, half-eccentric atmosphere surrounding its publication.

ii

Beatrix Potter had always, perhaps as a result of her lonely and unnatural childhood, sheltered herself behind an immense reserve; and when, in early middle-age, she found herself modestly famous, she retreated into her privacy almost in alarm. Some shyness, some sense of personal inadequacy which had made her *gauche* as a girl, had clearly been the beginning of it. She dreaded strangers, and her father, by omitting as often as not to introduce her to acquaintances encountered at exhibitions, had sometimes made her wonder if he were ashamed of her. "I wonder why I never seem to know people," she had written with some misgiving when she was nearly thirty. "It makes one wonder whether one is presentable. It strikes me it is the way to make one not." But a great enjoyment of the *privateness* of private life was there as well, combining with her original awkwardness to drive her into a seclusion which had all the appearances of eccentricity, but which was essential to her nature. On marriage she had adopted her new name with the alacrity of one who for years had longed for the dignity of marriage, and also with the joy of a fugitive who stumbles on an unexpected disguise. She signed herself "Beatrix Heelis" to her publishers from that moment; *The Fairy Caravan*, in the private edition, is "by Beatrix Heelis"; and, as we have seen, she hated being addressed as "Miss Potter" by even the most appreciative of admirers.

Warnes had strict instructions never, on any account, to reveal her name and address to the inquisitive. Reporters from local papers, who realized who she was and naïvely decided on an interview, were met with blunt refusals or stupefying rudeness. So complete, except for the neighbourhood of Sawrey, was her incognito, that most of her admirers in her own country supposed that she was dead.

Strangely enough, this reserve was gradually softened and dispersed during the nineteen-twenties by visiting Americans, with whom, knowing her horror of publicity, one might have expected her to have been specially guarded. The reasons for this apparent inconsistency were, first, the serious and intelligent American attitude towards children's literature, and the flattering American appraisement of her own work; and secondly, the comforting sense of personal security conferred by the Atlantic.

The first American ladies who sought her out (but very delicately) in her retreat, and called on her, and wrote to her charmingly afterwards from New England addresses, were professionally interested in children's literature; Miss Anne Carroll Moore was then, and for many years afterwards, Superintendent of Children's Work in the New York Public Library, Miss Helen Dean Fish Children's Editor to a New York publishing house. Their professional descriptions make clear at once the serious American attitude towards children's literature, and to this Beatrix Potter immediately responded. "I entirely agree with you about English children's literature," she wrote to Miss Fish, after a congenial visit. "The authors used to write down to children; now they write twaddling dull stories or odiously slangy stuff. I thought your article in *The Horn Book* was excellent." And to Miss Anne Carroll Moore: "There have been classics such as *Alice in Wonderland* and *The Water Babies*, but in the main children's literature has not been taken seriously over here – too much left to the appeal of gaudy covers and binding, and the choice of toy sellers". (She seems, mysteriously, to have been quite unaware of her wonderful contemporary, E. Nesbit.)

From these new friends Beatrix Potter learned with interest that in 1916 a Bookshop for Boys and Girls had been opened in Boston, with a cultural as opposed to a commercial policy; and that its founder, Miss Bertha Mahony, had also launched a magazine, *The Horn Book*, entirely devoted to children's books and reading. Miss Mahony, who rightly regarded Beatrix Potter as one of the few genuinely great figures of children's literature, was added to her growing list of American correspondents, and, tactfully but persistently questioning on behalf of *The Horn Book*, did much to undermine her personal defensiveness. "There have been two letters recently from Miss Bertha Mahony of the Boston Bookshop," Beatrix Potter wrote in 1925 to Anne Carroll Moore. "The letters which ask for particulars about 'Beatrix Potter' are very perplexing. I have a most intense dislike to advertisement. (And I have got on quite well enough without it.) On the other hand, a mystery is silly, and it invites curiosity. And I object to being supposed to be the wife of Sidney Webb, a member of the late Socialist government. He married a Miss Beatrice Potter – no relation. There were photographs of him in the newspapers, it said his wife had written children's books." Reassured by Miss Moore she gingerly, and as though each word might loose on Sawrey an avalanche of the odious "trippers" she detested, set down for Miss Bertha Mahony some crumbs of fact.

To the travelling Americans who came to see her she was open and friendly, and there is no doubt that she got a great deal of pleasure from their acceptance of her books as nursery classics. "Never," she wrote to Miss Mahony, "does anyone outside your perfidiously complimentary nation write to tell me that I write good prose." (It is curious that she should have received this tribute with such pleasure, when she was stung to rudeness by the equivalent suggestion that her pictures were good art.) In the warmth of this discriminating admiration she unbent, and even (a thing she had never attempted before) tried to analyse her own method of writing. "I think I write carefully because I enjoy my writing, and enjoy taking pains over it. I have always disliked writing to order; I write to please myself ... My usual way of writing is to scribble, and cut out, and write it again and again. The shorter and plainer the better. And read the Bible (unrevised version and Old Testament) if I feel my style wants chastening."

By contrast with the respectful attentiveness of her new friends she formed, somewhat unjustly, the impression that she was less intelligently appreciated in her own country. She could not deny her overwhelming popularity with English children, nor her incomparable sales; but she had an irritated feeling that while the New England ladies prized her as a beacon of culture, her English publishers looked on her chiefly as an investment. This was unfair, for she had rigidly refused for many years to have any personal contact with either publishers or readers in her own country, and Warnes, in confining themselves to the briefest of business letters, and always warning off admirers who tried to discover her address, were faithfully carrying out her expressed wishes. As a result, her American admirers seemed to be far more numerous and congenial than her English ones; they arrived in a gentle, steady, deferential stream during the summer months, bearing letters of introduction, and were received cordially; while the few native tourists in the Lakes who discovered her identity, and came for a curious peep over the garden wall, were usually less fortunate. "A good many Americans arrive," she wrote to Mrs. Charles Hopkinson of Cambridge, Massachusetts, the wife of the painter, "we had a very pleasant party of friends from Boston to tea a few weeks ago." On the other hand, the few English visitors who claimed acquaintance with her were, she considered, "very inquisitive, and completely uninteresting. However it happens, the class of Americans who take the trouble to call, are quite different from the English." This special feeling towards her American public goes a long way to explain what otherwise would seem an eccentric action on the part of so English a writer – the decision to withhold from English children her longest and most personal book.

iii

The Fairy Caravan, as she suspected, is not good work, though there is charm, and feeling, and humour in many parts of it. It is a big story-book in which all the left-overs, the unfinished fragments and the experiments of her later years have been pressed down together and given some appearance of unity by a connecting thread of narrative. It is a time-honoured device for linking together a collection of unattached tales, and Beatrix Potter employed it – loosely and carelessly enough, and not very successfully – to gather into one book all the loose threads of story and fancy about her farm animals and the animals of neighbours which she had invented to amuse herself over a period of years – Tuppenny, the long-haired guinea-pig that she had bought on one of her rare visits to London after her marriage ("I bought a carpet and a guinea-pig, both extortionate in price") and who looked, with his long hair, so fabulously oriental, like a little Sultan of Zanzibar; Sandy, the dog next door; her own sheepdogs; Dolly, her little pony who "loved water", and who always, when crossing a stream, "stopped the pony cart and had a good splash"; the flocks of Herdwick sheep which had become the centre of her farming life, and whose hardy, lonely existence on the high fells had stirred her imagination.

Her own poultry, all tame as pets and individually known to her, are here given the honourable mention that she felt their characters warranted. As long ago as 1910 she had written to one of her child correspondents, "Do you think *hens* would make a good story? At my house in the country I have got some white fowls which are such dears; they will let me pick them up and stroke them. Some people say that birds are uninteresting, but *Jemima* has done next best to *Peter Rabbit*," and her later letters are scattered with affectionate references to her poultry. "I am very fond of Silver Campine fowls. They have more character than the general run ... Their bright dark eyes are more expressive than the snaky gold and black stare of the usual barndoor hen ... Henny-Penny, the mother of Charles" (the domineering cock of *The Fairy Caravan*) "was a wonderful layer, and she laid immense white eggs. I could always pick out Henny-Penny's eggs in the basket – but the difficulty was to find them! I think Jemima Puddle-Duck might have taken a lesson from her in the art of hiding nests." In *The Fairy Caravan* her Campine fowls, "Tappie-tourie, Chucky-doddie, Selina Pickacorn, and five other hens", have a rambling winter night's adventure – not with Mr. Tod this time, but with John Stoat Ferret. It does not compare at all with *Jemima Puddle-Duck*, but it is not without its own discursive attraction.

The caravan which gives the book its title houses a little circus troupe of animals, who travel (invisible to humans) in the neighbourhood of Sawrey and the surrounding hills, performing to other animals in farmyard and field. Beatrix Potter had always had a passion for travelling circuses, never missing one in the Lakes if she could help it. "Went to see Ginnet's Circus at Ambleside," she wrote in her journal in 1895, "and had a good laugh. I would go any distance to see a Caravan (barring lion-taming); it is the only species of entertainment I care for." When the animals in *The Fairy Caravan* camp, they pass the time in telling stories, and it is in the form of tales told by first one and then another of her characters that she fits in any fragment or story that cannot be made a part of their own adventures. Taking the book as a whole, (which it is not easy to do, it is such a patchwork) one sees at length that its happiest moments are all concerned with the little unpretentious animals – the mice, guinea-pigs, Jenny Ferret, the cats and rats; and that all its weakness is due to that elderly loss of critical sense and discipline which allowed her to be in turn discursive and high-flown, to introduce personal references of purely local interest, and even some deplorable fairies. "You asked," she wrote some years later to Mr. Samuel Cunningham, a Senator of Northern Ireland with whom, in the last years of her life, she kept up a correspondence, "you ask why I have never written about dogs. I *have!* but I could not do them justice. I can manage to describe little rubbish, like mice and rabbits – dogs, sheep and horses are on a higher level." It is, indeed, the "little rubbish" characters of *The Fairy Caravan* that give it value, half smothered though they are among much that is tedious and profuse; and the story of Tuppenny the guinea-pig (whose hair grew and grew, although "Mrs. Tuppenny cut it, and cut it, and stuffed pin-cushions with it, and pillow cases and bolsters") is the one story in the book in which her old tender, sure, ironical spirit is distinguishable.

If the tale of Tuppenny had been written in the years when Beatrix Potter still had the self-discipline to prune her work down to the exquisite minimum, and sight clear enough for painting guinea-pigs as ravishingly as they appear in *Appley Dapply* and *Cecily Parsley*, we should have had a delicious addition to the nursery bookshelf. As it is, *The Fairy Caravan* is not to be despised. Children love it; and if they are bored by some chapters, and indifferent to others, they still take an uncritical pleasure in the rest. It is not, to tell the truth, a book which can be enjoyed at all in a critical spirit. It is not good enough. And yet to dismiss it as a failure is to deprive oneself of the pleasure of some charming things. "Through many changing seasons," Beatrix Potter wrote in the little preface, "these tales have walked and talked with me. They were not meant for printing ... I send them on the insistence of friends beyond the sea."

iv

Sister Anne and *Wag-by-Wall*, which also belong to this period and were published in America, are of little interest except, perhaps, to the curious or the book collector. Beatrix Potter had always had a fondness for the idea of re-telling nursery rhymes and fairy tales in different guises: she had done it with complete success in *Jemima Puddle-Duck*, but in *Sister Anne*, that long and wearisome re-telling of the Bluebeard story which was "pruned away" from the structure of *The Fairy Caravan* by David McKay, she was struggling hopelessly against the current of all her capabilities. Varlets, barbicans and palfreys dismally abound; there is not one natural touch in the book, not one gleam of vitality anywhere to suggest its authorship; it is a pretentious failure.

Wag-by-Wall, on the other hand, is modest enough. It, too, was produced when Beatrix Potter was long past illustrating her own work, and it has no pictures. It is a simple story such as any grandmother might tell a child, about a poor old woman who finds a fortune in the toe of a stocking. It has no animal characters, no trace of freshness or humour, no evidence of life; only a kind of quiet prettiness and pathos. "I cannot judge my own work," she wrote to Miss Mahony, sending her this little story; ". . . I thought of it years ago as a pendant to *The Tailor of Gloucester* – the old lonely man and the lonely old woman; but I could never finish it."

For *Little Pig Robinson*, published by David McKay hard upon the heels of *The Fairy Caravan*, Beatrix Potter looked through her old notebooks and rough sketches, and came across *The Owl and the Pussycat* and the pig that had gone to sea in the *Pearl of Falmouth*. (She had begun a story about this pig as long ago as 1893, but had discarded it because "the story stuck on board the *Pound of Candles*.") It is much longer than her earlier books, (excepting *The Fairy Caravan*), and one must confess that it is very dull. *Pig Robinson*, however, as "the new Beatrix Potter", was a sufficiently attractive proposition for Warnes (who had, indeed, been puzzled and hurt by what seemed an inexplicable breaking away from her old publishers) to ask if they might publish it in London under their own imprint. Beatrix Potter agreed, and *Pig Robinson* appeared simultaneously in England and America, being issued from Bedford Street like his elders and betters.

CHAPTER
EIGHT

Mrs Heelis of Sawrey

i

It is rare for old age to be the happiest period of life, but there is no doubt that in middle age and after Beatrix Potter found a satisfaction and contentment that she had never known in youth. She had, as the foundation of her quiet existence, a happy marriage; she was embedded in the simple life she loved, sending down manifold roots into what she believed by heredity to be her native soil; and she had the satisfaction (vital to one of her temperament) of labour that was not only "real", but useful. She built herself in, she all but fortified herself in her life in Sawrey; and there, through thirty years, projecting her ideas and leaving her beneficent imprint on the countryside, gradually became that endearing and formidable person, in appearance not unlike Mrs. Tiggy-Winkle, whom the countryside in its turn came to appreciate and love.

Life at Castle Cottage, as the Heelises lived it, was plain and comfortable – law books and papers and deed-boxes at one end of the dining-room table, bramble jelly and toasted teacakes at the other. There were no tiresome concessions to appearance. "Mrs. Heelis I like very much," Miss Choyce wrote home to her mother, when her offer of war-time help on the farm had been accepted and she had been installed at Hill Top; "she is quite out of the common ... short, blue-eyed, fresh-coloured face, frizzy hair brushed tightly back, dresses in a tweed skirt pinned at the back with a safety-pin ... Mr. Heelis is a quiet man, very kind. They believe together in the simple life."

Simple it was indeed, and unpretentiously comfortable – the very opposite of the life the Potters had always led, and which Mrs. Potter, now a widow, still scrupulously followed. Rupert Potter had died at eighty-one after a "miserable illness", within only a few months of his daughter's marriage. His last years had been difficult for everybody. "If my papa has a fault," Beatrix wrote guardedly when she was twenty-six, "he is rather voluble in conversation, and though not such a dragon as Edwin Lawrence, he is oppressively well-informed." His dragon qualities had gathered weight with age, when irritability had increased with physical suffering. Only here and there in the journal do we find complaints, but it is clear that his irascible temper was a burden. "I should have enjoyed it more without papa and the flies," she wrote in 1894, after a drive on the Northumberland moors, and the words "as usual, deplorable", occur with depressing frequency in connection with her father. "My father being troubled with gravel again, and every prospect of a hard winter, I have become lower than is the habit with me, a cheerful person ... Must confess to crying after I got home, my father being as usual deplorable." Medical advice had been strong for their wintering abroad, or at least in Falmouth, but "I only fear papa will refuse to move before he is ill. I am anxious to do my best, but I really cannot face going abroad with him." The pain he suffered (particularly, it seems, on Sundays, before going to chapel) was often "shocking"; nothing relieved it but "an extraordinary amount of morphia." "He was never very patient of discomfort," Beatrix wrote to Millie Warne after his death, "and his trials were very great." There remained the problem of Mrs. Potter, bereaved, solitary and unoccupied in Bolton Gardens, and now doubly at a loss, since both her children were gone. "She will miss him dreadfully; they had been so constantly together, and with few outside interests." It was thought best, especially in view of the war and the danger from Zeppelins in London, that she should come to the north and take a small furnished house in Sawrey, with her only surviving sister-in-law for company. "It is the best plan," Beatrix wrote cheerfully to her old friend; "and I tell William it is highly complimentary to *him* that these old ladies take refuge in the neighbourhood; but it does keep *me* on the trot. I have had rather a hard summer."

The four years of the war passed quietly enough, all things considered, at Castle Cottage. William was keeping his law office running on a short staff, and acting as special constable; Beatrix was always busy about the farms, hoeing turnips, getting in the hay, increasing and learning to use her farm machinery, turning her hand to anything that needed doing. The wife of the forester on the neighbouring Graythwaite Estate remembered that "when food was scarce during World War I he came upon her one wet cold November day gathering acorns in the woods for her pigs. She had a shovel and a wheelbarrow for the job, and was fit up to brave the weather in a short thick wool skirt, a man's jacket and cap and a sack over her shoulders ... She was on the Graythwaite side of Esthwaite Lake and would have to wheel that heavy barrow up a long steep hill home just to give the animals she loved a treat." In

1918, a few months before the armistice, her brother Bertram died suddenly in Scotland. Peaceful, painless and totally unexpected, his death was a great shock, both to Beatrix and her mother. "I shall miss my brother sadly," she wrote to Millie Warne, mourning him as an ally and supporter; "we seldom met, but we wrote regularly . . . and we could help one another." And to Canon Rawnsley, "I don't think I yet realise that Bertram is gone – in his prime, and in his usefulness . . . I do think he found true happiness in hard useful manual work . . . He is buried like the Grasmere folk in the bend of a stream – a flowery graveyard with a ruined ivy-grown church, and graves of the Covenanters."

It was a sad year; Bertram gone, the war seeming as though it might go on for ever, the precious harvest ruined by bad weather; a year for enduring and remembering losses. "This might have been a sorry and ashamed letter," she wrote to Millie. "I lost Norman's ring in the cornfield – pulled off while lifting wet sheaves with my fingers slipped under the bands; but it turned up amongst the remains of some wet stuff thrown down for the hens. I had untied many on the threshing floor in hopes of finding it. I am glad I was spared that last crowning distress . . . I should have had just one consolation, it was a pretty, quiet, sheltered field to lie in, if it had not been found. My hand felt very strange and uncomfortable without it."

The war over, it was thought best that Mrs. Potter should not return to London, and even – revolutionary decision – that number Two Bolton Gardens should be given up. Instead, she would make her home at Lindeth How, one of the large secluded grey granite Victorian houses on the other side of Lake Windermere which the Potters had rented occasionally in earlier summers, and which required a sufficient number of servants for Mrs. Potter, in her solitude, to feel at home. Beatrix supervised the removal of furniture from London to Windermere, and installed her mother (as upright and fresh-complexioned in her eighties as she had ever been, and marvellously unchanged) with her needlework and canaries in the new drawing-room window.

It was not an easy move, and Beatrix, being at this time not fully recovered from an attack of bronchitis, surprised her mother by a faint suggestion of impatience. "The goods arrived at Lindeth How on Tuesday; another three days of unpacking. The only drawback is that my mother has not been as well as usual . . . I do not think the arrival of her furniture was very good for her; though she sat in one room and watched through the window, it was a bit tiring and exciting." And a few days later, "I am about sick of that furniture – what with my mother asking for things I never saw, and various disappointments, it seems like a variation of the Prayer Book – 'I have brought the things I ought not to have done, and left the things that etc.' " But another month of hard work was necessary before Mrs. Potter was settled. "Got piano upstairs!" Beatrix wrote, in a spirit of triumph and exhaustion, in a letter to Miss Choyce; "my mother still searching at present for title deeds and several sets of old teeth and a black bag and a book of Braille writing and various other things . . ." But the translation of Mrs. Potter and her belongings had at last been accomplished, and she was able to resume at Lindeth How the life that death had so rudely interrupted in Bolton Gardens; to spend her mornings at embroidery, to lunch at one, and drive out each afternoon behind the coachman. And since this is perhaps the moment for taking leave of Mrs. Potter, it may as well be recorded that she lived in seclusion there until the age of ninety-three, with faculties unimpaired, and her way of life, with its punctuality and scrupulous observances, undergoing hardly any modification. "My mother is ninety-one and very well," Beatrix wrote to her cousin Caroline Clark in 1930. "I wish I were as little troubled as she is. If she gets a cold it is only a sniff – and I have been in bed twice this winter already. She is very lucky in having good lungs, no rheumatism, and good eyesight." And in 1932, finding herself at last answering letters of condolence, she wrote to Mrs. Rawnsley, "My mother's long life was a link with times that are passed away, though still vivid in our memory – the old leisurely pleasant days of stately carriage horses, and of the Keswick coach. Latterly she has lived so retired that modern changes have not much affected her. Her chief interests were her canaries, her needlework and her little dog. She was wonderfully clear in mind, but . . . I am glad that she is at rest."

ii

A little before she had brought her mother to spend her last years at Windermere, Beatrix Potter had made a bold purchase. At the time of her marriage she had been the owner of three small farms in Sawrey – Hill Top, Castle Farm (where she lived) and Courier – as well as a good deal of cottage property; and for the next ten years she had devoted herself to the slow, traditional, patient and practical work of learning to be a farmer. This she had done with great success, having brought to the task a shrewd eye and a retentive memory, and in everything concerning animals that quick practical response which is more fruitful than theory. Now, in 1923, Troutbeck Park, a wild and lonely fell farm estate of over two thousand acres, with a solitary stone farmhouse at the head of the valley and a stock of many hundreds of "heaf'd" or home-bred sheep, came into the market; and her means having increased very considerably since Mr. Potter's death, she ambitiously bought it.

This was the beginning of her long interest in Herdwick sheep, the little hardy blue-fleeced pretty-faced mountain sheep indigenous to the fells. From the first moment of seeing the native fell flocks, which had bred among the high crags – so far as anyone knew – since before the Stone Age, their ancient hardihood touched her. "Cool is the air above the craggy summit," she makes the old sheep say, in the story which was to become a chapter of *The Fairy Caravan*; "clear is the water of the mountain keld ... What though the tempest sweeps the fell in winter – through tempest, frost or heat, we live our patient day's allotted span. Wild and free as when the stonemen told our puzzled early numbers; untamed as when the Norsemen named our grassings in their stride. Our little feet had ridged the slopes before the passing Romans. On through the fleeting centuries, when fresh blood came from Ice-land, Spain or Scotland – stubborn, unchanged, *unbeaten* – we have held the stony waste." This lonely farm, covering the Troutbeck valley and the surrounding heights, now became the centre of her farming life, providing strong draughts of space and solitude, nourishing her imagina-tion. It was about twelve miles from Sawrey, but in any weather her car might be seen winding along the valley road, or her short stout indomitable figure making its way on foot slowly and alone to the top of Troutbeck Tongue or

Lowther Brow, where the goat-footed flocks were feeding along the crags. She would spend whole days alone on the hills like this, eating her bread and cheese under a boulder, or, if it rained, at "High Buildings", a stone shelter that the lambing-time shepherds used. "Troutbeck Tongue is uncanny; a place of silences and whispering echoes. It is a mighty table-land between two streams. They rise together, north of the Tongue, in one maze of bogs and pools ... They meet and unite below the southern crags, making the table-land almost an island, an island haunted by the sounds that creep on running waters ... From the highest point of the Tongue I could look over the whole expanse; Woundale and the Standing Stones; Sadghyll and the hut circles; the cairns built by the stone men; the Roman road; Hollilands and Swainsdale, named by the Norsemen; and the walls of the Norman deer park stretching for miles." "In the calm spacious days that seem so long ago," she wrote, a little before her death, "I loved to wander on the Troutbeck fell. Sometimes I had with me an old sheepdog, Nip, or Fly; more often I went alone. But never lonely. There was company of gentle sheep, and wild flowers and singing waters." Sometimes strange things happened in the solitary places. "Another time all by myself alone I watched a weird dance ... It was far away in that lonely wilderness behind the tableland on Troutbeck Tongue. In the midst of this waste of yellow bentgrass and stones there is a patch of green grass and a stunted thorn. Round the tree – round and round in measured canter – went four of the wild fell ponies. Round and round, then checked and turned; round and round reversed; arched necks, tossing manes, tails streaming. I watched a while, crouching behind a boulder. Who had taught them? Who had learned them to 'dance the heys' in that wilderness? Oftentimes I have seen managed horses cantering round the sawdust ring under a circus tent; but these half-wild youngsters had never been handled by man ... While I was watching them I remembered how I had been puzzled once before. In a soft muddy place on the old drove road I had seen a multitude of little unshod footprints, much too small for horses' footmarks, much too round for deer or sheep ... The finding of those little fairy footmarks on the old drove road made me first aware of *The Fairy Caravan*."[1]

She was capable of watching animals for hours, herself as still as a stone, and in the hard grey tweeds of her own Herdwick wool looking no more remarkable on the bare hillside than a squat lichenous boulder. "I once saw a curious proceeding on the part of a dog ... I was on a hillside, looking down on a lonely track up the valley. An old terrier belonging to a neighbouring farm appeared coming down the track, at a businesslike steady pace by himself. He either did not see me or took no notice. He crossed a foot-bridge into a field where he behaved very oddly – zig-zagged about for several short turns and then deliberately dived off a bank into a deep pool in the beck. He did not splash about; he stood in the bottom of the pool so long that I thought that the dog was committing suicide. It then came out for a breather, and dived in again. It was not fishing. It afterwards went on its way homewards ... I believe it is a fact that confirmed sheep-worriers have the brains to wash themselves, and they do not worry sheep near their home. It was a curious proceeding to watch from the steep hillside overhead. The dog was so deliberate, and the water in the pool so clear; he just stood in the bottom."

[1]This description was printed in *The Horn Book*, May, 1942, and is reproduced by kind permission of Miss Mahony.

Her sheep she watched, followed, tended and understood, coming down from the hills to the lonely farmhouse
to talk to the shepherds; to handle the long hard polished
wooden crooks that they still used; to attend the dipping,
standing in clogs by the pens in the carbolic-streaming
yard; to watch the marking of the sheep with brands dipped
in tar – making the "tarrie woo" which in the handloom
days had made the Herdwick wool so hard to card and
spin. She had in her temperament that blend of the
practical and the poetic which is so often found in
shepherds; above all, perhaps, in men of mountainous
districts. She respected their skill, and learned to understand it, bringing her masculine intelligence to the problems of hill-sheep farming; and she loved the simple idiom
of their thought and speech, which was often striking and
profound, and of great beauty. "There is something very
lovable about the silly sheep," she wrote to Samuel Cunningham, "and the simple old-fashioned talk of those that
work the soil and the flocks ... Do the shepherds in
Ireland say of a pining sheep, 'It's doubt if she will ever
hear the cuckoo'?"

There was drama, to her, in the life of the Herdwick
flocks, which was not shared by the placid sheep of the
low pastures. They climbed, like chamois, up to the
inaccessible places, were "crag-fast" sometimes, when the
rock had crumbled behind them, unable either to go up
or down, enduring days of sun and thirst, "eating the grass
to the bone, parched by the sun and wind", before they
died or were rescued. Sometimes, when blizzards overtook
them as they came down from the fells, they were buried
in the drifts, and crowded there, packed together under
the frozen vault, for a week, a fortnight, sometimes three
weeks and more, patiently nibbling the moss and their

THE TALE OF BEATRIX POTTER

own wool, until the sheepdogs found them – "dogs scratching, and shepherds prodding the drift with the long handles of their crooks." There was poetry in the compulsion that these native ewes felt towards their own "heaf", the hilltop where they were born, and the long journeys back they would make over the fells, if they were sold away; and poetry, too, in the risks the shepherds ran, in snow and dangerous high places, and their long nights in the cold and dark at lambing time, and their tenderness and patience. The little sheep themselves, sturdy and small and smoky-blue, with strong thick forelegs and tiny hooves, were more beautiful than ordinary sheep and more endearing. Their rams had fine curling horns, and battled each other when they met, and stamped and defied the dogs with lightning movements; the ewes were intelligent and nimble; the lambs had a nursery-rhyme prettiness, and kittens' faces.

The dogs at work with the shepherds were themselves an ever astonishing and absorbing study – a race that seemed to hand down through its generations a knowledge and tradition altogether apart from the lore the shepherds taught them. Beatrix Potter had her own favourite dogs which she trained herself, teaching them as puppies to drive and round up the long-suffering poultry in her yard before she tried them out on gathering sheep. Her own favourites, unlike the shepherds' dogs on the farms, had the freedom of the house, and were usually a part of the comfortable muddle of her fireside, toasting against the fender with Mr. Heelis's slippers.

Sheep farmers and shepherds as a class are jealous of their experience and traditions; they do not welcome the newcomer, and they despise the theorist. But Beatrix Potter – or Mrs. Heelis, as she was now widely known in the Lakes – they did accept; there was no gain-saying her knowledge, and they gave her a place among them without reserve. It was now, in the nineteen-thirties, that she became a familiar figure at all the sheep fairs in the district – a very odd figure sometimes, if the weather were bad, bundled up in many layers of tweed, with a stick in her hand, metal-shod clogs on her feet, and some nameless covering over her venerable head. She would appear as spectator, exhibitor, judge, going critically round the sheep-pens with one of her shepherds – Tom Storey of Hill Top, George Walker or Anthony Benson of Troutbeck, Tom Stoddart of Tilberthwaite; absorbed and intent, speaking the same speech, and utterly indifferent to appearance. Her strange clothing sometimes amused even herself, when she had been made aware of its oddity by some innocent reaction, and the Crompton in her, now fully developed and as crusty as even old Abra'm himself could have wished, took a singular pleasure in despising convention. She was fond of telling the story herself of the tramp who had met her in wild weather, toiling up a drove road to look at her lambs, in her usual rag-bag attire with a sack on her head and shoulders, and who had called out in fellow-feeling, "It's sad weather for the likes o' thee and me!" And she had been "touched and amused" by the compliment paid her by some gipsies (who in Cumberland go by the name of "tinkers" or "potters") who, noticing that at country sales she showed a "curious taste for old iron-trivets, crooks and such like –" and supposing from her name and appearance that she was one of them, offered her (if she "would not bid against the gipsies") an "invitation to join the potters' inner select auction ring."

So long as she could live and look like a farmer, she asked no better; and if it was regarded as eccentric by some of the gentlefolk round about, with whom she was on civil though wary terms, the farmers and shepherds respected her practical ability. "The high fell farms are not very suitable for land girls," she wrote when she was seventy-six and worried by the call-up of men for military service; "dear me! it makes me wish I were thirty years younger – I cared nothing for snow and ice." Nor did she: and, as one would have supposed, she was not squeamish. The pests and diseases afflicting sheep were the subject of her most earnest enquiry; she herself invented a trap (which was to be used in large numbers on the fells) for the detestable maggot-fly. "I am sure it would pay to tackle the *blue-bottle*," she wrote to Mr. Cunningham, "instead of so much dip and supervision of suffering sheep and lambs" – a suggestion typical of her surprisingly modern and scientific attitude to age-old problems.

As she increased her experience of hill-farming, and showed herself a serious and useful member of the Herdwick Sheep-Breeders' Association, the farmers of the district came to accept her as an authority. "I am in the chair at Herdwick Breeders' Association meetings," she wrote, with mingled amusement and satisfaction, to Miss Mahony. (It was the first time in the history of the association that the chair had been taken by a woman.) "You would laugh to see me, amongst the other old farmers, usually in a tavern, after a sheep fair." At these meetings the problems of Herdwick breeders were discussed (specialized problems unknown to those who breed for soft wool and for mutton) produced by harshness of climate and terrain, and by the fact that the hard-wearing Herdwick wool, once in great demand for drugget, was losing its market. "Briefly," she told Miss Mahony, "our Herdwick sheep with their *hard* waterproof jackets are the only sort that can thrive on the high fells; but the demand for their wool almost ceased when linoleum came in and carpets went out of fashion." Some new use, she hoped, would one day be found for the tough bluish-grey wool of the little Herdwicks, for "the poor sheep have to be shorn in summer", and it seemed there was no other use for the barren stony wastes of the high fells where the Herdwick sheep had bred and thrived for centuries.

Her love for the sheep, and the work that she did for this ancient and little-known breed, was fully recognized in the sphere where she valued recognition – among her fellow farmers. Hers was an opinion most seriously sought at sheep fairs and sales, hers a voice respectfully listened to at farmers' meetings. She is remembered and regretted among them, not as the Beatrix Potter whom the world knows, but as Mrs. Heelis of Sawrey, president-elect of the Herdwick Association and one of the shrewdest farmers in the Lake Country.

iii

The best achievement, however, of this last period of Beatrix Potter's life is undoubtedly the work that she did for the National Trust. The seed which Canon Rawnsley had planted in her mind in girlhood had struck deep, and he would have rubbed his hands in glee (as he had zestfully rubbed them in life over many a lesser triumph) if he had seen its fruit. No one, not even Wordsworth, had loved the Lakes more passionately than the Canon; and being a practical man, with a fine fund of energy, he had expressed in a lifetime of constructive work the emotions which a more lambent imagination would have turned to poetry. (He had tried to express it in poetry as well, but verse with him was rather a habit than a vocation.) He saw clearly – as Beatrix Potter was in her turn to realize – the special dangers menacing the Lake District. To the natives of the fells and dales it was a farming country, difficult but in some ways rich, and of a strongly traditional character. It had also, by virtue of its great beauty and the wildness and grandeur of its high places, a value which not even the native farmer had a right to debase. But the farmer, though he was capable of small vandalisms, was not the enemy. Because of its wild beauty and easy accessibility from the industrial cities of the north, the Lake District was in constant danger of being turned into a spoiled tripper-ground by people whose very gusto for the place was considered an excuse for the horrible things they did to it. More damaging still, with hopeful fingers pressed on the tourist pulse, there were those sordid forces which throve on what is called "development" – the buyers of building sites and throwers-up of bungalows, the char-à-banc and box-lunch companies, the setters-up of tea shanties, the promoters of serviced motor roads across the solitudes – in short, all those wide-awake concerns which thrive on other people's love of the country by making the country totally unenjoyable. It was a delicate problem: how to preserve the beauty and agricultural integrity of the Lake District, so that it should refresh the minds of all who came to it, and be accessible to all; and at the same time to control the tourists, parasites, who were so short-sightedly bent on destroying those very beauties and solitudes that attracted their hosts.

Canon Rawnsley saw what he (and Beatrix Potter after him) believed to be the best solution, in the acquisition of as much Lakeland property as possible by the National Trust. Big private landowners, though they were often good landlords to the farmers and kept the jerry-builders and ribbon-developers at bay, were unreliable from the point of view of preservation; with the best intentions in the world they died or went bankrupt; they might be good while they lasted, but there was no security. And the small farmer, though one might feel he had as good a right to his native fell as the bigger one, was even less satisfactory. If he did not fail, and sell out his road frontages to the highest bidder, he was apt to contribute his innocent bit to spoliation. "Small-holders are hopeless," Beatrix Potter wrote in despair to Mrs. Rawnsley; "first they sell off all sheep stocks; and then they cut all timber, and concentrate on hens . . ."

The National Trust as landlord had many advantages. It paid neither income tax nor death duties, and could therefore afford proper repairs and maintenance. It had the advantage, too, that it pleased very nearly everybody: it was benevolent to the farmer, sympathetic (though admonitory) to the tourist, and watchfully jealous of all the beauties under its protection. The only persons, in fact, who disliked it were those very types it was created to defeat. The Trust, however, had its own difficulties, chief of these being that it depended for every penny that it spent on public subscription. For each acre bought, it had to raise public money, and support by the same means its own fairly heavy expenses of organization. For every purchase there were public appeals, and though as a rule these were adequately met, they sometimes failed; the funds subscribed would be too small, and the Trust and its supporters would have the anguish of seeing some stretch of coast, some historic house or incomparable view broken up or sold to the despoiler.

With the aims of the Trust, and especially with its policy of preservation in the Lake District, Beatrix Potter was in perfect sympathy, and soon after her marriage she began to subscribe money towards its various projects – sometimes under her own name, more often anonymously. She began, too, to regard her own acquisitions in land in a more perpetual light. In the beginning, when she had bought Hill Top Farm, then a few fields, a handful of cottages, a wood, a quarry, it had been purely to satisfy a personal hunger; now she saw that she might be the instrument of protecting these fields and woods and hillsides permanently. She bought now, as Canon Rawnsley would have done if he had had the means, with an eye on the Trust, snapping up likely bits of local property; and in this her husband, as a family solicitor of long standing in the district, discreetly possessed of innumerable estate secrets, was a great help to her. "I have been much gratified," she wrote to Caroline Clark, "to get back the bit of land at Tilberthwaite that belonged to my great-grandfather Abraham Crompton. I should have liked to keep it for my lifetime, but on the whole it seemed wiser to make a gift of it to the National Trust when they bought the surrounding property." "For years I have been gradually picking up land," she told Samuel Cunningham when she was seventy, "chance bargains, and specializing on road frontages and the heads of valleys. I have a long way towards three thousand acres ... It is an open secret it will go to the Trust eventually ... I own two or three strikingly beautiful spots. The rest is pleasant peaceful country, foreground of the hills, I think more liable to be spoilt than the high fells themselves."

In 1927 a strip of foreshore and woodland near Winder-mere Ferry came into the market, and the Trust appealed for funds. Beatrix Potter had already given as much as she could afford, and having failed to charm a handsome donation out of her mother ("I *do* regret she has been so awkward about the Trust and money") she conceived the idea of selling original sketches through Miss Mahony's Boston Bookshop for Boys and Girls, and sent a packet of fifty signed drawings, each to be sold for a guinea. It was a laborious way of earning fifty guineas (far more so than the Christmas cards which she designed each year for the Invalid Children's Aid Association, her favourite charity) but she grudged neither time nor trouble in the work which was, in a sense, her spiritual bequest from Canon Rawnsley, and which she undertook for the most part so anonymously that her full share in the preservation of the country they both loved can only be guessed.

It was in 1930, in the course of amassing the scattered small properties that she intended for the Trust, that she was able to perform her most valuable (though severely practical and unspectacular) service. The large Monk Con-iston estate, stretching from Colwith Bridge to Carrs, and southwards to the village of Coniston, came into the market, and to keep it from being broken up or "devel-oped" she bought it immediately, offering at the same time to re-sell half of the property to the Trust and to retain the other half of it only for her lifetime. This practical piece of preservation was done as unobtrusively as possible, but by no means meekly, for in nothing was the Crompton streak in Beatrix Potter's character more thornily revealed than in her dealings with the Trust. She was not "giving" these fine properties to the nation, though she was making it possible for the nation eventually to possess them, and she was quick to snub any compliment to her generosity. "I have read today the report of the annual meeting," she scolded in 1932, "and I am exceedingly annoyed about it. The announcement about Thwaite Farm, in direct contradiction to my expressed wish, was quite gratuitous, when two other acquisitions were described as anonymous . . . Willie and I had made up our minds to give a good deal more if my mother had died last time when she was so ill. *Now I won't*." But of course she did; and when her mother's death had solidly increased her means the anonymous help (seasoned with very vigorously expressed opinion) went on even more generously. In the end, she admitted to Mr. S. H. Hamer, the Trust's wise and tactful secretary, "the things I have had to miss are a vexatious remembrance. However – I am glad I had the pluck not to miss Monk Coniston."

The work which she undertook for her beloved countryside was not confined, however, to money loans and shrewd buying for the Trust. She managed, on behalf of the Trust, much of the farm property which she bequeathed to it, and in the last ten years of her life undertook whatever seemed to her most useful – from tree planting to picking up paper bags. (Trippers' litter, of course, was one of the heartbreaks of the work, and the consumers of box-lunches in beauty spots seemed to regard the Trust's tactful litter baskets rather as a stimulus.) Nothing was too small for her attention. A tree which ought to be felled; another which should be preserved because of its proportion to the landscape; a roof to be slated or a gate mended, a farmhouse which the tenants were not keeping clean; a dealer who was going off with the heavy carved oak cupboards "riven out of ancestral cottages" – not one of these details was allowed to escape the searching gaze which many people found so disconcerting, or to go unreported in her copious letters. By her will, the Lake District holdings of the National Trust were increased by four thousand acres, which included Troutbeck Park, Tilberthwaite, her "dear farms and the sheep", and many smaller holdings and cottages which she had restored to good condition: for in Beatrix Potter the National Trust had not only a benefactor, but a loving caretaker, who had once, long ago, expressed with brush and pencil what she felt about the high hills and the valley farms of Cumberland and Westmorland; and who now took comfort, in her old age, from seeing at least a few of them preserved from ruin.

iv

Rosy-cheeked even in her seventies, old age became her like a bloom. She was not afraid of it, nor saddened by it, but added a little frilled white cap to her attire when she considered it proper, accepting, as her grandmother Jessie Crompton had done before her, the goffered badge of decorous old-ladyhood. "I do not resent older age," she told her cousin Caroline; "if it brings slowness it brings experience and weight ... It is a pity the wisdom and experience of old age are largely wasted." And a few years later, reflecting on the slipping away of the years, she still maintained, "I mind it little – with one or two reservations. For one thing (to quote a friend) 'Thank God I have the seeing eye' – that is to say, as I lie in bed I can walk step by step on the fell and rough lands, seeing every stone and flower and patch of bog and cotton-grass where my old legs will never take me again. Also", she asked, her

Crompton voice suddenly audible, "do you not feel it is rather pleasing to be so much *wiser* than quantities of young idiots? . . . I begin to assert myself at seventy." Work, not ease, was the secret of contentment; keeping the tools in one's hand. "I would rather keep going till I drop – early or late – never mind what the work is, so long as it is useful and well done." "I am sometimes surprised at myself, being contented," she told Samuel Cunningham in the last year of her life, "I lift my eyes to the hills, and I am content to look at them from below. I did dream of getting an old pony (or a donkey) but I think I am safer pottering about on my own old legs . . ."

These last ten or fifteen years had been full of rewards. The loving companionship of married life had meant much, and if it had come late, it was all the more dearly prized. ("I married very happily . . . What are the words in *The Tempest*? 'Spring come to you at the farthest, in the very end of harvest . . .' ") Her occasional odd ferocity, her blunt speeches and silent disconcerting stare – "the searching, expressionless stare of a little animal" as someone has described it – were never directed against her beloved William, who was always respectfully consulted (however she might choose to act) and treated with deference. At an age when many people grow indifferent they had drawn more closely together, and below the surface of their most practical, unsentimental life there was a romantic current, the understanding gentleness of lovers. One catches the atmosphere of it, never explicit but always present, in innumerable letters. "Today, Tuesday, is a hot and windy day again, we shall soon be hay-making if this intends to last. Yesterday evening was the first really warm night. William and I fished (at least I rowed) till darkness; coming down the lane about eleven. It was lovely on the tarn, not a breath of wind . . . I see the first rose is coming out at Hill Top . . ."

Her feeling for Hill Top had grown stronger, if anything, with the years. Nobody lived there now; she went often alone, walking slowly across the Post Office meadow with her two Pekingese at her heels, to work in the garden or wander about the house, opening the windows, peacefully rummaging among her old furniture and china and the accumulated relics of her life. Samuel Whiskers no longer visited Hill Top, and the Cannons had retired years ago and gone to Stavely; but nothing else was changed. There were still Mr. Warne's bellows, and the cups and saucers she had drawn for *The Tailor of Gloucester*, and the plum-coloured curtains that had hung at the landing window in Tabitha Twitchit's day. Only the rooms were perhaps a little more crowded than they used to be, for she had never got over her fondness for country sales, and her purchases of old oak – farmhouse cupboards and chests and coffin-stools and presses – were more numerous, even taking into account the number of her cottages and farms, than they really should have been.

It distressed her to see the heavy carved oak cupboards "riven out of ancestral cottages", where they had originally been built into the thickness of the wall, and subjected to the indignities of the sale room. They were one of the native beauties of the Lakeland farms, and in the seventeenth and eighteenth centuries had been carved with love by the farmer and his sons; wherever she saw them exposed for sale she bought them, and put them back – with almost a sense of a decency performed – where they belonged. "The local furniture of this region was oak; rather out of fashion in the sale-rooms now, but I collect any genuine pieces I can get hold of to put back in the farmhouses.

The court cupboards with the carved fronts are the most interesting ... It is a great shame to take them out of the old farmhouses, for they really don't look well in a modern room ... I am 'written out' for story books," she told Miss Mahony, "and my eyes are tired for painting; but I can still take great and useful pleasure in old oak – and drains – and old roofs – and damp walls – oh, the repairs! And the difficulty of reconciling ancient relics with modern sanitation!" She understood the physical harshness of life on the fell farms, especially for the women, and in the early 'thirties had taken the practical step of helping to found a Hawkshead and district branch of the Nursing Association. There was, strangely enough, much "overt opposition" to this scheme, and she zestfully dominated the early committee meetings. "I congratulate you," she wrote to a fellow committee member, "on your speech, which was concise, to the point, and marked by a dignified reticence which is always conspicuously wanting in the orations of your present correspondent." The opposition to a salaried nurse was successfully crushed, being chiefly, it appears, from "old women who went out 'to oblige', and their relations, who were all offended on their behalf," and so many farmers' wives for the first time in their lives had the comfort of skilled nursing in childbirth. "I might have told them," she wrote in a letter, "that a big strong young married woman died of pneumonia three years ago near the back of Tilberthwaite. The neighbours still say regretfully, 'She was thrown away ... we did not know what to do for her.'" Managing the finances and the quarrels – "There is only too much jealousy between villages" – brought out the triumphant Crompton in her, since she did not in the least mind reducing the committee ladies to tears by her "scathing remarks" (as one of them remembers) "on their slack ways . . . She was much loved – also much disliked – but never ignored."

She had the strongest feeling that the farms and cottages of Cumberland and Westmorland belonged to the people of the dales, and would never let one for holiday purposes, or to "offcomes". "My house property," she declared in her will, "shall continue to be let at moderate rents to the same class of tenants as heretofore, and . . . my farms shall be let at moderate rents to good tenants." By good tenants she meant, among other things, natives; since they were the only people with any right to those white-washed, slate-roofed dwellings; and to those (they were not many) who had the temerity to recall that she herself had been an "offcome" once, and had been born in London, she would turn a face of genuine surprise – that "countenance full of intelligence and humour", as Delmar Banner, who painted her portrait, has described it, "in which all that is most direct, dignified and engaging in childhood and old age seemed to meet" – and gravely explain that that had been "a mistake". She had come to identify herself so closely with the people of the dales that she often spoke, and seemed to think, in dialect; even in letters, if she were writing to a farmer, or Joe Moscrop, the "lambing-time man" who came each year with his shepherd dog from Scotland, she would lapse unconsciously into their tongue, and write blithely that "the heifers have calved easy", or "the last potatoes took up a disgrace."

She hated change, but rather in the way of loving and regretting the good things of the past than with the peevish prejudices of old age. She delighted in the singing games that the young women of Sawrey remembered from childhood, and which they would often go through for her at Christmas, standing round the piano. She loved to watch the country dancing which was still – not so very long ago – kept up, and recruited teams among the girls of the village, and bought them dresses for competitions and festivals. She had never danced herself, and was now too old; but "W.H." had been an athlete in his day and was still lean and nimble, and not above dancing a set of "Newcastle" to shame the younger ones, while his wife looked on and laughed and patted her lap, and said it was a dance "one never tires of". There were other country relics, too, of the receding past, which had not quite disappeared, and which she dwelt on fondly: "I thought of our singing games last Saturday when I was in Keswick, and heard some little girls puzzling out a half-forgotten skipping rhyme...."; and the village boys, with their "pace-eggin'" song at Easter, not comprehending at all these last fragments of the ancient mumming, but coming always to Castle Cottage with their ritual tom-foolery because they got smiles and shillings from Mrs. Heelis –

> "Here's one or two jolly boys all of one mind;
> We've come a pace-eggin', I hope you prove kind;
> I hope you'll prove kind with your eggs and strong beer
> And we'll come no more nigh you until the next year."

And when the two of them were alone in the winter with the lamp on the table, there was the fascinating labyrinth of Crompton genealogies to be pored over, and obscure paths to be explored, leading a little nostalgic way into the past; and the yellowing Stuart napkins to be taken out from the cupboard and examined, and those curious cipher

MRS HEELIS OF SAWREY

manuscripts of her own, written "long ago, and in another world", when she had sat drawing butterflies at the library table at Camfield Place, her eyes on her book and her whole spirit drinking in her grandmother.

v

In the anxious days of 1939, a few months before the outbreak of war – the third war of her lifetime – she began to fail, and it was soon clear that she would have to undergo an operation. She faced it, and the possibility of death, with simple calm. To Miss Margaret Hammond, niece of the beloved Miss Hammond of her childhood, who for years now had been her next-door neighbour in Sawrey and a trusted friend, she admitted that the bad news had been "not entirely without premonition." She had failed in strength, these last two years, "more than people know ... Most times it has been an effort to walk to Hill Top. I am so glad I was feeling particularly well last week, and have seen the snowdrops again. If it were not for poor W.H., I could be indifferent to the result. It is such a wonderfully easy going under; and in some way preferable to a long invalidism ... Moreover, the whole world seems to be rushing to Armageddon." ("But not even Hitler," she added obstinately, "can damage the fells ...")

She set her affairs in order and made her will, taking care that her house and farm servants were all remembered; making it clear that her Herdwick flocks were to be kept by the National Trust on their native "heaf"; and that "hunting by otter hounds and harriers shall be forbidden and prohibited over the whole of my Troutbeck property",

195

and the walled garden and wood at Belmount Hall, a house she had inherited, kept as a bird sanctuary. The copyright of all her works she bequeathed first to her husband, then to the favourite nephew of Norman Warne. That done, she turned her mind to Hill Top, still dearest refuge and symbol of first freedom, and the manifold little relics and treasures which it was harder to think of as scattered than all her more valuable properties. As she had kept it for more than forty years, so she wished it to remain; unchanged; not lived in by other people. She knew exactly how she wanted the china always in the cupboards, and where her great-grandfather's Bible and *Gerard's Herbal* and a particular candlestick were to stand, for ever: and lay propped in bed with pencil and paper, writing minute directions. She could not lie easy until her mind had dwelt in peace on that inner vision.

But she had not seen the last of Hill Top, for her wonderful stamina, which had carried her about the hills in all weathers and had set her to work in garden and field and farmyard at an age when other old ladies doze beside the fire, was to bring her home to Sawrey, reprieved but still secretly failing, to live through four more busy and harrowing, but undiscouraged years. "I am incredibly well," she wrote to her cousin, just before war broke out, ". . . and can do a bit of weeding when it is not too hot. Thank you for the kind enquiry – I bide some killing!"

She and William tackled their wartime problems in practical fashion, without heroics. "I was never afraid of housework or outdoor work," she told Miss Mahony. The shortage of help, inside the house and out, was soon to take its toll of the ailing and elderly, but for the moment she faced the future without misgiving, and her north-country blend of the practical and the poetic stood her in good stead. ("I am provoked to have missed the Aurora," she wrote to Mrs. Delmar Banner, when one of those beautiful luminous curtains had been seen in the north during a January night; "Wm. and I were in the cellar with a candle, salting two pigs' legs.") Soon William was appointed to the county War Agricultural Committee, and as well as his work as solicitor and Clerk to the justices, was "going round farms, surveying for next season's ploughing – an invidious job amongst neighbours." Evacuees meantime flowed in like a tide from Tyneside and Newcastle – "It is said there is not an apple left in Windermere" – and the tide of young farm labour drained away. "I enjoyed a bit of field labour yesterday, picking up turfs in the oat field, but had pains and stitches and aches afterwards – too old!"

Sawrey was "safe" from air raids, but not entirely spared those incidents which seemed to befall even the remotest communities – bombers burning out on the fells, sheep and cattle destroyed, a lonely farmhouse and its inmates obliterated by a wandering raider – and the sky was "red with fires, night after night." These lurid skies, appalling as they were to contemplate, had a grim beauty. "I shall always remember seeing tracer shells like rockets beyond the Langdale Pikes in a frosty night ... But for the knowledge of its cruelty and suffering, a raid at a distance is beautiful, with searchlights and flares."

To the kind Americans whose embarrassed letters arrived in Sawrey while England was hourly threatened with invasion she answered much as old Abra'm might have done, with an odd unconscious suggestion of one of her own characters (Mrs. Tiggy-Winkle, surely?) thinking of leaving her known burrow for a while. "One thing is certain, *I* shall not run far. I will retire into the nearest wood" – to Mr. Tod's wood-shed, possibly – "the cellar of course for bombs; but it is one in a million risk. If there is invasion, I am afraid villages near the landings will be burned. I look wistfully at my fine old furniture. I have a wonderful old bedstead too heavy to move in a hurry." (Or is it Hunca Munca speaking?) "Nevertheless I went to a sale at Coniston the other day and bought three chests and a coffin stool. Two of my chests are thin and long, like deed boxes. They might come in convenient in the wood for holding things, dry and solid ..." "Did I ever tell you," she asked Samuel Cunningham, "I used to know an old Highland woman who remembered the fear of 'Boney', and the little ploughed patches among the hills? ... Let's hope we live to see the end of it. I am kept up by strong curiosity to see what happens next."

There was plenty to eat, though the fare got plainer and plainer; and wood to burn when coal was scarce; besides, Beatrix Potter had an old-fashioned liking for a large number of flannel petticoats, and cocooned herself against the northern cold. For her Christmas dinner with William in the third winter of the war she had "a (hutch) rabbit, and a tiny bit of pork, which Mr. Heelis prudently salted." Wild rabbits, the favourite stand-by of the little dogs, had mysteriously disappeared. "The Pekes had the satisfaction of catching one of the last survivors. They are quite plump themselves. They eat a good deal of potatoes, plus gravy and gristle, and do not despise MOUSE."

It was her last Christmas. The fourth winter of the war found her weary, though she would not confess it, and William, too, worn down with work and worry and the comfortless daily fatigue which was punishing the old. "Everyone is getting tired; Wm. is so tired and getting deafer ... But he does not feel he can retire from the office . . . I have managed all right as regards farming – sitting up in bed in a nightcap, interviewing shepherds! I wish I had not broken down just now . . ." She had caught a cold, and it had turned to bronchitis; the weather was bitter, and she was compelled to stay in bed. This she did, but not patiently at first; feeling there was so much to be done; sitting up in her little woollen nightcap to hear about the sheep, and give instructions; writing copious letters; arranging with the Scotch shepherd about the Troutbeck lambing; conning the weather from her bedroom window; incorrigibly putting down cracker crumbs for the mice who gnawed so impudently in the wainscot; brooding over the news . . . "I hope to do a bit more active work yet – and anyhow I have survived to see Hitler beaten past hope of recovery." But her life's work was finished, and suddenly, a few days before Christmas she found herself, calmly and without self-pity, engaged in the final struggle. Almost her last conscious act, while she remained aware of the season of the year, was to write a faint message to the old friend and shepherd who had come to her every lambing time for sixteen years. "Dear Joe Moscrop . . . Still some strength in me. I write a line to shake you by the hand, our friendship has been entirely pleasant. I am very ill with bronchitis. With best wishes for the New Year . . ."

Beatrix Potter died on the twenty-second of December, 1943, at the age of seventy-seven. She died as she had lived, as simply as possible, conscious of what she was doing, without fuss or regret. To the end she was aware of the beloved companion at her bedside, and she looked her last by daylight, gazing as long as she was able on the spare wintry outline of the hills. "Sorrows of yesterday and

today and tomorrow" – did she remember her own words? –
"the vastness of the fells covers all with a mantle of peace."

APPENDIX

THE BEATRIX POTTER BOOKS
(Published by Frederick Warne & Co Ltd, unless otherwise stated)

1 The Tale of Peter Rabbit (privately printed)   1901
   (The first privately printed (flat-back) edition, 250 copies, Dec. 1901, was followed by a second privately printed (roundback) edition, 200 copies, Feb. 1902.)

2 The Tale of Peter Rabbit   1902

3 The Tailor of Gloucester (privately printed,   1902
   500 copies)

4 The Tale of Squirrel Nutkin   1903

5 The Tailor of Gloucester   1903

6 The Tale of Benjamin Bunny   1904

7 The Tale of Two Bad Mice   1904

8 The Tale of Mrs. Tiggy-Winkle   1905

9 The Pie and the Patty-pan (first published in   1905
   the larger size format)

10 The Tale of Mr. Jeremy Fisher   1906

11 The Story of a Fierce Bad Rabbit (Panoramic   1906
   Form)

12 The Story of Miss Moppet (Panoramic Form)   1906

13 The Tale of Tom Kitten   1907

14	The Tale of Jemima Puddle-Duck	1908
15	The Roly-Poly Pudding (first published in the larger size format, and in the smaller size as *The Tale of Samuel Whiskers*, 1926)	1908
16	The Tale of the Flopsy Bunnies	1909
17	Ginger and Pickles (first published in the larger size format)	1909
18	The Tale of Mrs. Tittlemouse	1910
19	Peter Rabbit's Painting Book	1911
20	The Tale of Timmy Tiptoes	1911
21	The Tale of Mr. Tod	1912
22	The Tale of Pigling Bland	1913
23	Tom Kitten's Painting Book	1917
24	Appley Dapply's Nursery Rhymes	1917
25	The Tale of Johnny Town-Mouse	1918
26	Cecily Parsley's Nursery Rhymes	1922
27	Jemima Puddle-Duck's Painting Book	1925
28	Peter Rabbit's Almanac for 1929	1929
29	The Fairy Caravan (privately printed, 100 copies)	1929
30	The Fairy Caravan (David McKay, Philadelphia) (First English edition, July 1952)	1929
31	The Tale of Little Pig Robinson (David McKay, Philadelphia)	1930
32	The Tale of Little Pig Robinson (first published in the larger size format)	1930
33	Sister Anne (David McKay, Philadelphia)	1932
34	Wag-by-Wall (limited edition, 100 copies)	1944
35	Wag-by-Wall (The Horn Book, U.S.A.)	1944
36	The Tale of the Faithful Dove★ (limited edition, 100 copies)	1955
37	The Art of Beatrix Potter (reproductions of her drawings and paintings)	1955

38 The Tale of the Faithful Dove (F. Warne & Co. Inc., New York)   1956

39 The Journal of Beatrix Potter, 1881–1897 (transcribed from her code-written manuscript)   1966

40 The Tailor of Gloucester – a facsimile of the original manuscript and illustrations (limited edition, 1500 copies, F.Warne & Co. Inc., New York)   1968

41 The Tailor of Gloucester – from the original manuscript (F. Warne & Co. Inc., New York)   1968

42 The Tailor of Gloucester – from the original manuscript (the English edition)   1969

43 The Tale of the Faithful Dove – with illustrations by Marie Angel (F. Warne & Co. Inc., New York)   1970

44 The Tale of the Faithful Dove – with illustrations by Marie Angel (English edition)   1971

45 The Writings of Beatrix Potter – a history of, including unpublished work   1971

46 The Sly Old Cat   1971

47 The History of the Tale of Peter Rabbit   1976

48 The Magic Years of Beatrix Potter   1978

* This slight tale, without illustrations, was written by Beatrix Potter in 1907, but never published in her lifetime.

HILLTOP

Beatrix Potter's original Lakeland home, Hilltop, Sawrey, which features in so many of her books is now National Trust Property and is open to the public during the summer months.

INDEX